Enigma of
LEAN

Demystifying Mysteries of Lean

I0510285

N C NARAYANAN

INDIA · SINGAPORE · MALAYSIA

Notion Press Media Pvt Ltd

No. 50, Chettiyar Agaram Main Road,
Vanagaram, Chennai, Tamil Nadu – 600 095

First Published by Notion Press 2021
Copyright © N C Narayanan 2021
All Rights Reserved.

ISBN 978-1-68563-332-5

Contents

Part – I
Lean Thinking

Part – II
Methodology of Lean

About the Author

NC Narayanan, fondly known as 'NC', is the Founder Chairman of SSA Business Solutions (P) Ltd, a global management consulting company head quartered in India. He founded SSA in 1999 with a personal mission to transform Indian industries to world class – a goal that he has pursued passionately throughout his career spanning more than five decades. NC travels across the globe sharing his experience in various forums. As a CEO coach and mentor for leadership teams, NC has made significant contributions to hundreds of industries and thousands of individuals across Asia, Middle East, and Africa where he has earned the reputation of a 'Transformation Catalyst'.

He is a voracious reader and also author of many books. The most popular one is *"PRAGMATIC LEADERSHIP"* published by McGraw Hill Education which was well received for Human resource development. In this book NC shared many tips for developing leadership skills through Personal, Teams & organizational leadership in progression. This book has been translated in regional language of India recently. Apart from self-development topics, NC has authored many management topics such as *"ENIGMA OF LEAN"*, *"SIX SIGMA IN A NUTSHEL"* and *"STATISTICAL GUIDE"*. He is an avid blogger who shares his knowledge & wisdom through many subjects in social media covering spirituality, Music, and many leadership development topics. His YouTube channel has many of his resources for public consumptions.

NC is a Gold Medallist in Mechanical Engineering, holds an MS (Research) degree in Computer Aided Design from the prestigious Indian Institute of Technology popularly known as IIT. He has also done his management program on Change Leadership.

NC's Resources:

1. Pragmatic Leadership:
    https://www.youtube.com/watch?v=
    FhlOrLPxIYk&list=PLpHHSPrdvzCEFQGWObXD573QlrKe
    b8eUs

2. Theory of Happiness:
    https://www.youtube.com/watch?v=
    ZLMKmT4pQSM&list=PLpHHSPrdvzCFPemxUa7SJEex2v8
    yXQ2h4

3. Meditation & Spirituality:
    https://www.youtube.com/watch?v=
    Jpc8xANOUvY&list=PLpHHSPrdvzCExTi_8AINNTv_oA-
    Ac9F0-

4. Learn Music with NC:
    https://www.youtube.com/watch?v=
    R-s4Q6rJA0Q&list=PLpHHSPrdvzCFbt66uIQKIw6rk7kqGeO9G

5. Profit leadership:
    https://www.youtube.com/watch?v=
    nl4upoEPbBw&list=PLpHHSPrdvzCG4FvKmJIl2uP8Mn6
    VLTHjh

6. Lean Thinking:
    https://www.youtube.com/watch?v=_Hi_
    vCgOFzo&list=PLpHHSPrdvzCEbh9GsCSanjjDp1tpwlsr9

7. Pragmatic Leadership book:
    https://www.amazon.in/
    Pragmatic-Leadership-Unleashing-Leader-within/dp/
    9385965646/ref=sr_1_1?crid=2XXT1Z9YX9F5G&dchild=
    1&keywords=pragmatic+leadership&qid=1631031382&sr=8-1

Reviews by Business Leaders

Karan Singh,

Managing Director, ACG

"I am captivated by the 'Enigma of Lean' and recommend this book to all leaders striving to keep their organizations dynamic and agile. Best wishes to NC for this new book"

R S Subramanian

Senior Vice President & Managing Director, DHL Express India.

"There is nothing basic about basics" is what we say in DHL – to highlight that 'getting basics right' needs attention and discipline. This book captures the basic concepts very well and rich in content with examples to clarify the fundamental principles of LEAN THINKING & CONTINUOUS IMPROVEMENT (CI).

NC in his characteristic style explains lucidly the history, philosophy, and business relevance of Lean & CI. There is something in this book for everyone – business leaders, change agents & consultants to pick up, practice and achieve breakthrough results in their enterprise.

Sayyid Nasr Albusaidi

General Manager (Customer Experience)

Oman Post & Asyad Express, Oman

"I thoroughly enjoyed reading this book reflecting my own personal experience as a 'Transformation Leader' over a decade of driving business excellence in Oman. I am one of those fortunate ones who listened to NC's thoughts personally during his visits to Oman. Through this book, NC poured his practical wisdom gained over 5 decades of orchestrating major transformations projects in India and other countries.

This book covers the pragmatic approach to Lean instead of theory which can aid business leaders, tactical level people and consultants to use Lean as a vehicle for transforming the entire organization to achieve a competitive edge. I highly recommend this book as a reference guide to business leaders, students and consultants"

Abbas Jamal

CEO, Al Hassan LLC, Muscat, Oman

"In the current economic crisis Lean can be a life saver as I have personally experienced its application for recovery, consolidation & excellence of any enterprise. In this book NC covers everyone's needs such as CEO's, CXO's and change leaders at tactical levels. The uniqueness of this book is it answers Why, What & How aspects of Lean as a transformation strategy"

Jagdish Gandhe, Executive Vice President – Manufacturing & Technologies,

Piaggio Vehicles Pvt. Ltd

This book is a great reference for understanding the LEAN "Methodologies" and "Tools and Techniques" to implement the same. Moreover, the latest edition is having value added information to the LEAN practitioners on how to bring sustainable improvements to organisations, while transforming the organizations by adopting LEAN philosophy.

Jayanandhan Vasudevan, Supply Chain Professional, DKSH, Myanmar

"Enigma of Lean unravels the concepts of Lean in an extremely effective manner. NC has outlined the concepts with very good tools and techniques, would recommend this book to all emerging leaders"

Dr. Raju Desai

Chairman, Jyoti Group

The need of the hour of global enterprises is paradigm shift as the Pandemic rewritten all the rule of the game drastically. To achieve India's vision to reach 5 trillion economies, all enterprises must become world-class right from MSME to corporate. Lean provides a means of achieving this as it covers the Strategy – Structure – Systems (3S) all at the same time.

NC is known for his abundant knowledge and simplicity of making complex subjects easy to learn. Through this book he has provided a cook-book approach to Lean implementation simultaneously demystifying all myths of this great science. I wish him & all entrepreneurs a great success through Lean systems & culture.

Shridhar Gokhale

Director & CEO, Indo Tech Transformers Ltd. Kancheepuram (TN)

"Mr. NC has commendably demystified the word "Lean" and explained it in simple words. This book brings clarity on related philosophy, tools and methodology which will be helpful to beginners and existing practitioners alike. A must read for everyone at any phase of their career"

David Hampton

Partner at Advanced Analytics Solutions LLP, United Kingdom

"This book clearly explains not just the tools and techniques of Lean but also the underlying philosophy and management thinking that is needed. It shows a clear path to success for the enterprise. Well done NC!"

James O'Neill,

Founder and MD of Career Path Recruitment Ltd, Ireland

"NC, through the 'The Enigma of Lean', has created an outstanding reference resource for anyone who wishes to take a holistic approach for implementing the concepts of "Lean". This book is an essential guide for organizations undertaking the journey to adopt a 'Lean Philosophy'.

Dr. Obiora Madu,

CEO, Multimix Academy, Nigeria

"My first understanding of Lean was from NC. I went through the first edition of this book, and it was fantastic. The one under review is a massive improvement on the first edition. I have seen that Lean is capable of reviving ailing organizations. That was demonstrated in a lean project in Nigeria where NC promised 25% reduction of cost but after the project, that was exceeded substantially. This whole experience is what I see in this priceless book. I recommend it to both leaders and every professional who wishes to assist their organization realign and reduce costs"

Foreword

Diego Graffi

Chairman & Managing Director

Piaggio Vehicles Private Limited

The human civilization has constantly endeavored to discover better ways of living, which sets it apart from other creations. The discovery of gravity by Isaac Newton in the 1600s and other discoveries that followed laid the foundation for the Industrial Revolution of the 20th Century. Since then, several scientific inventions have occurred that have led to the development of a number of products that invaded our daily lives. This transition occurred in phases – 'Industrial revolution', 'Electronic revolution', 'Information revolution' and now the 'Internet revolution' – all of which have changed our lives. All these developments have also led to increased complexity in technology and the resultant complexity in industries.

Gadgets such as automobiles and aircrafts were invented in the early 20th Century, and they revolutionized our transport systems. They also brought many complexities to the design and manufacturing processes. As the automotive industry grew in the 19th Century, it faced a unique challenge of mass-producing motor cars to meet the burgeoning demands of the growing middle class; and with no exemplar companies to model their manufacturing systems and supply chains against, they had to look for innovative solutions. The advancement of the industrialized era over the decades have been chronicled in the form of *"Industry X.0"* for each stage of advancement e.g. the current new wave of connected and smart manufacturing is coined as 'Industry 4.0' and the early systems of motor car and aircraft manufacturing as 'Industry 2.0', and predating this, invention of steam engine (circa 1765) as the first 'Industry 1.0'. The Industry 3.0 & 4.0 are led by automobile companies to remain at the forefront of cutting edge technology.

As the automotive industry evolved, quality control became a central issue and subsequently cost consciousness, which led to companies competing to become the lowest cost producer. As competition grew from emerging players in Europe and Japan, the incumbent players in the industry had to be on their toes to stay relevant and compete. They banked on continuous innovation and improvements in product design and manufacturing methods. The customer expectations of better features and shorter lead time for delivery warranted innovation in R&D and manufacturing systems to produce First Time Right (FTR) products with zero defects.

Due to the foregoing challenges, automobile industries have been at the forefront of innovation in product design, material science, supply chain practices, manufacturing system's engineering and other management practices. In fact, they were the early adopters of the teachings of The Quality Gurus like Dr. Edward Deming and Dr. Joseph Juran thought leadership and ideologies creating constantly learning and changing organizations. Among the many transformation ideologies adopted by automobile companies, 'Lean' is the most significant of all that revolutionized the way the entire automotive value stream functions today.

"Lean Manufacturing" (which owes its roots to The Toyota Production System) is the integration of many best practices that have revolutionized the way manufacturing can be efficient and effective. Lean is not just a set of tools or techniques (as it is typically misrepresented), it is a holistic philosophy grounded in time-tested principles that helps to design the most efficient value stream. Another misconception of Lean is that it is merely a manufacturing system, the truth is, it is an ideology that helps eliminate waste from any business process and achieve steadfast focus on delivering customer value as promised. The principles of Lean can apply to any business model apart from manufacturing including trading, contracting, services and manufacturing.

The author, NC Narayanan (fondly known as NC) rightly titled this book as 'Enigma of Lean' as his main intention of writing this book to demystify lean for the benefit of business leaders and consultants worldwide. He passionately believes that Lean is a transformation vehicle through which an enterprise can re-discover itself and create a powerful competitive advantage. I have known NC for many years as a mentor and passionate transformation catalyst. He brings rich experience gathered over 50 years working in automobile and ancillary industries and later on in management consulting. He served in many corporate leadership positions and later founded his consulting firm with a missionary zeal to transform enterprises through new paradigms. NC has helped many industries embrace Lean principles both in manufacturing & service sectors across several industries worldwide and achieved breakthrough results. In this book, he reflects on his vast experience both as a practitioner and a scholar in this subject. He has endeavored to highlight many pitfalls and challenges one may face during their lean transformation journey.

NC highlights that Lean is fragmented and applied as a tool for point optimization while it is a holistic system optimization principle. Many a time, it is applied as a bottom-up approach using tools such as 5S, Kaizen, Kanban, TPM etc. in most of the industries, which does not lead to breakthrough results. The reasons for such failure include the lack of holistic understanding of Lean and the non-availability of a structured methodology to apply Lean for a value stream transformation. NC argues that while Six Sigma benefited from the DMAIC Framework for problem solving, Lean has no such widely practiced framework. To fill this gap, NC has proposed a new methodology for lean application called RMAOR (Recognize – Map & Measure – Analyze – Optimize – Repeat).

NC wrote the first edition of this book in 2015 and it was intended only as pocket book for limited circulation for his clients and students. In this edition, he has expanded it as a "cook-book" for Lean implementation with a very systematic approach methodology. He has presented the book in two parts – Part-1 explains the philosophy of 'Lean Thinking', which is aimed to educate the business leaders and board of directors to know what Lean is and how it can help to enhance ROCE from their business and position themselves with a competitive advantage. In Part-2 of the book he explains the RMAOR approach of Lean transformation with the appropriate tools & techniques to be used in each phase. To summarize, this book covers "Why Lean?" (Part-1) and "How to apply Lean?" (Part-2). I personally feel that this book will provide a reference guide for those who are decision makers of enterprises, change leaders and consultants who will benefit by the 'How' part of Lean implementation. NC also covers the pitfalls of change management based on insights he gained from his years of corporate leadership and global management consulting.

This book is a must read for any visionary leader considering to embrace Lean principles in their enterprise and I wish this book all the success!

Prologue

In the history of human civilization, this planet has witnessed a dramatic growth in technology which has resulted in complex business models. In the last three to four decades the information technology has revolutionized the way in which organizations function. It also has resulted in many complex service organizations such as Business Process Outsourcing (BPO's) and Knowledge Process Outsourcing (KPO's).

These organizations have posed a bigger challenge for the management to optimize its resources and remain competitive. In addition to the complexity of the organization, the globalization has brought world-class products and services to the consumers demanding very cost effective and value adding products. The industries are under cost pressure than before challenging the traditional mind set of passing on the cost to the consumers. Hence the business leaders are under constant pressure to remain profitable and grow.

The concept of quality that was applicable a century ago is no longer valid. The product quality, although important, it alone does not provide the competitive advantage an organization may be looking for. The concept of quality has been continuously evolving or expanding due to the thought leadership of many quality prophets like Dr. J.M. Juran & Dr. Edward Deming.

In the words of Dr. Edward Deming, it is no longer **business of quality** (product quality) which is alone important but, the **quality of business** that matters for differentiation. The Quality of Business refers to the 'Quality of Thinking' from the Board Room that is driving the organization through leadership, aligning people through

Purpose, Vision, Values and Strategic directions up to the grass root levels. The urge for continuous improvement with the involvement of the people has helped many organizations to achieve prosperity of un-precedented levels.

The organizational development for achieving competitiveness focuses on three aspects as given below:

1. Increasing the speed of all responses

2. Elimination of waste of all kinds

3. Alignment and the involvement of the people for continuous improvements.

In the last few decades, the two major philosophy and tools revolutionized the industries performance are Lean and Six Sigma. Lean focused on improving the velocity of the product manufacture whereas Six Sigma focused on variation reduction and hence defects.

Primarily the waste results from underutilization of resources or by producing defective products and rectifying them. By eliminating waste, the organization becomes effective by delivering its commitments to its customer at the lowest price and achieves customer loyalty.

In order to increase the speed of response, Taiichi Ohno from Toyota motor company founded the branch of improvement science called LEAN in the year 1960. In order to eliminate waste, the Lean philosophy added many tools and techniques as the lean approach evolved over the last 40 years.

Lean challenges the traditional way the products are manufactured in batch processing often called 'Push system' which accumulates lots of inventory and have long lead time for delivery. Lean also known as 'Flexible manufacturing system' or 'Pull system' reduces inventory and lead time substantially as it manufactures to the customer order through continuous flow from raw material to finished goods.

In the words of the Taiichi Ohno:

"All we are doing is looking at the timeline from the moment the customer gives us an order to the point when we collect the cash. And we are reducing the timelines by removing the non-value-added wastes"

– Taiichi Ohno 1988

As the Lean commenced its journey from Japan, very limited knowledge transfer could take place because of the language barrier till 1980. Subsequently many organizations in the west have attempted to develop the body of knowledge on Lean in English which has resulted in many fragmented resources in the form of concepts, tools & techniques. Unlike the Six Sigma which has been fitted in the DMAIC (Define-Measure-Analyze-Improve-Control) structure which has facilitated easy learning and application, the lean did not have the benefit of such a structure.

In order to fill this gap, SSA Business Solutions Pvt Ltd (SSA) proposed the RMAOR (Recognize-Measure-Analyze-Optimize-Repeat) methodology, which will facilitate easy learning and application of Lean to both manufacturing and service organizations. This book is titled '**Enigma of Lean**' with an intention to demystify the mystery or the myth of lean and encourage industries to make good use of this powerful intervention. This book aims to document the synopsis of RMAOR methodology for easy reference by the Lean professionals. Each step in the RMAOR is briefly explained along with the tools & techniques and examples wherever applicable. This book aims to provide a reference handbook for the Lean professionals as they teach and consult for Lean manufacturing and service processes.

This book has been written with an ambitious aim to help those who wish to know the subject of "Lean Thinking" as a philosophy aided by methodology and tools & techniques. It shall act as a cookbook reference guide for those Lean practitioners to apply systematically to transform their industries value stream. The business leaders who wish to transform their organization through Lean as a vehicle will be benefitted by knowing why it is the right approach.

With the above aim in mind this book is written like a textbook rather than compiling the tools along the methodology. You will also find examples along the methodologies which will provide a lucid learning for the reader who is introduced to the topic of Lean first time. This book has been written in two parts while part-1 answers 'What is Lean & why it improves profitability?'; the second part explains the RMAOR approach with step by step roadmap and tools & techniques that can be applied in each step.

The structure of the RMAOR methodology is presented with a roadmap at the beginning of each chapter followed by detailed explanation of the steps along with the tools and techniques. At the end of the guide, you will find a complete roadmap of the entire RMAOR methodology which will help the Lean practitioners to get the big picture of Lean and relate with the topics discussed in the various chapters.

This book is dedicated to all those who will believe in this 'Powerful tool' and create prosperity for their organization.

Wish you happy reading.

– N C Narayanan
The Author

Acknowledgement

The SSA Business Solution Pvt Ltd (SSA) team always demonstrated their eagerness to share their knowledge through as many media as possible and publication is one of them. I wish to record my sincere appreciation to the following contributions by those who supported me for publishing this book:

1. To Sashi Ganesh Iyer, my daughter and MD of SSA for driving me crazy to write many books. She has been the driver for many such contributions of SSA.

2. To my wife Meera who has been constantly encouraging me while I wrote this book during my vacation.

3. To my son Naveen Narayanan, MD of our middle east operations currently pursuing his Ph D in Lean in Buckingham University in UK for providing me lots of insights and latest updates on Lean Thinking.

4. To Quaidjohar for proof reading and re-creating images and arranging graphics for the excellent presentation of this book.

5. To Kushal Patel and our knowledge development team for assisting me in creating the new graphics for edition 2.

6. To all other people in my family & company who have been a source of inspiration for me to write this book.

7. To Ruchita Jalan who did the proof reading of this second edition.

8. Finally, the publishers of second edition with lots of enhancements from first edition.

Part – I

Lean Thinking

CHAPTER 1

Introduction

Why this book?

The first edition of this book was published in 2015 with an intention to demystify the concept of 'Lean Thinking' among the professionals & consultants and to aid the business leaders to make the right choices for their development of the organizations by applying Lean as an intervention. During the tenure of my corporate career in Lucas TVS in the early 80's, I was actively involved in the radical changes across all aspects of the value stream, including vendor integration, new product development, information flow and manufacturing systems. Although the term "LEAN" was not coined yet, all of lean's concepts were applied to break barriers for information & material flow to improve its velocity. The common man had difficulty in understanding why and what is happening in the organization as every function was undergoing major changes. When such a radical transformation takes place, everyone is worried what is this all about and how will it affect their position and stability? This posed a big challenge for the top management to communicate the need for change. Hence, the change leaders must design a comprehensive communication strategy to instill confidence among the people in the organization.

Although there are plenty of resources available to learn Lean tools & techniques, there were limited resources available to address What is Lean? Why Lean is to be applied and how to apply Lean in transforming an organization? Having worked in organizational transformation for more than five decades, I thought I will venture on filling this gap through this book. This book will answer all the three questions asked above and give a cookbook approach to apply lean for the entire organization or for a specific part of it.

Rationale for Lean

The Lean Thinking started in Japan through Toyota Production system (TPS) way back in 1950 with an intention to produce motor cars of highest quality with least cost. Toyota broke many myths about zero defects and flexible manufacturing. Although automobile technology came from the west, Japan broke all performance benchmarks through the application of new paradigms in which Lean & JIT (Just In Time) played a major role. The Japanese culture and attitude helped them to break all barriers due to their simplicity and humility. TPS (Toyota Production System) revolutionized the way in which an organizational value stream can be designed with least amount of non-value-added activities which is the main aim of Lean Thinking.

When we define the value delivered to the customer clearly, we can look at all micro-level activities under microscope to evaluate its ability to create value for the customer for which he or she is willing to pay. If any activity is not delivering value to the customer or erodes their value, it is termed as NVA (Non-Value-Added) activity. Systematic identification and elimination of NVA is the main aim of Lean Thinking. The subsequent chapters shall explain more details on how to apply Lean in a systematic manner.

Misconception of Lean

Like any thought leadership encounters the onslaught of abuses, Lean is not an exception. One of the reasons Lean was misunderstood was due to its big picture view and application. Unlike other concepts that came in the past like Six-Sigma are more local than global as Lean which is challenging the entire organizational value delivery as well as its business model. When the scope is large, it is liable for misconception. In this book I wish to demystify the fundamental philosophy, methodology and application of Lean tools in detail. Please stay till the end of the book to get the nine yards perspective of Lean before you choose to apply this wonderful concept which can revolutionize your business results.

The Big Picture of Lean

The following diagram (Fig 1.1) illustrates the big picture of lean Thinking which has three dimensions like the three corners of a triangle.

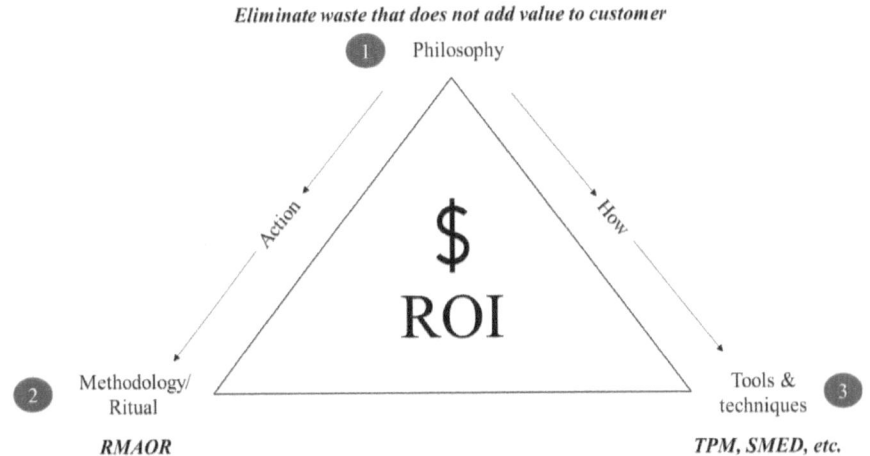

Figure 1.1: Big Picture of Lean Thinking

At the heart of the triangle, you will find dollar sign which denotes the main purpose of applying Lean to any enterprise which is enhancing profitability and customer retention. The sides of the triangle shows the connectivity of the three main aspects of Lean. The apex of the triangle explains the philosophy which is the belief on which Lean Thinking is built. The intent of Lean is to eliminate waste from the value stream to optimize cost and enhance value delivery to the customer. We have defined what is waste above in the previous section. The other two corners of the triangle are 'Methodology' & 'Tools & Techniques'.

The methodology is the systematic step by step way of approaching the value stream for improving flow by eliminating waste. The 'Tools & Techniques' are the tool kit which are handy to analyze a system through data. If the philosophy which is belief is not in place, the other two may not work. The main problem of many Lean applications is using the tools without any methodology and belief. This is the main reason the organizations do not get any lasting gains by the time and money they spend.

Drawing parallel to six sigma which has the following three aspects:

Philosophy (Belief) – Zero defect is possible

Methodology – DMAIC (Define – Measure – Analyze – Improve – Control)

Tools & Techniques – Many statistical tools

The six sigma approach was well accepted and understood as it was well structured with all the three aspects whereas, Lean came from Japan which was not well structured for public consumption. This is the main reason Lean was highly misunderstood and misused. Realizing this gap, I have proposed RMAOR methodology in 2015 through my first edition of this book. The first edition was published as a pocketbook which was very brief about RAMOR approach. Now in this edition, I wish to share my personal experiences and challenges in transformation gained over many global consulting across many business models such as manufacturing, trading, contracting and service.

Change & Transformation

Often these two terms are interchangeably used as though they are synonyms, while they are phenomenally different. A Change is local while transformation is holistic covering the entire organization; it is akin to 'Point Optimization' and 'System Optimization' which is detailed in the subsequent chapters. Change is incremental while Transformation gives breakthrough improvements. For example, if we re-engineer one process in the entire value stream, it is a local change which does not lead to a breakthrough improvement.

Many organizations choose one tool at a time such as six sigma and solve few process problems. Such approaches do not last long and yields only marginal improvements. Lean is a 'Transformation' ideology that can help the whole organization to be re-engineered for breakthrough improvements. Many automobile manufacturing companies have applied Lean across the entire value stream which covers the following business processes:

1. Vendor Integration to align vendors for Lean manufacturing systems as Green Channel vendors.

2. Forecasting, Planning & SCM systems applying DDMRP (Demand Driven Material Requirement Planning) principles.

3. Leaning the 'Information Flow' across all non-manufacturing departments.

4. Manufacturing system Re-Engineering in line with Lean principles.

5. Distribution network Re-Engineering aligning with DDMRP principles.

One of the reasons automobile and aircraft manufacturing have reached highest level of performance, setting benchmark is by the application of holistic Lean systems across all elements of the value stream. In terms of complexity as well as technology, these two industries cannot survive with traditional inefficiencies. Unfortunately, these Lean principles have not reached the rest of the industries although it is applicable to any business model including service and trading. I urge you to read through the entire book to get the pregnant power of Lean to improve the profitability as well as sustainability of any business model.

Why before what & how?

Right from the childhood our training & education starts with "WHAT" is to be done and then "HOW" to do it; we were never taught 'WHY' to do it. This applies to the organizational interventions where the business leaders wish to apply some tools & techniques because their contemporaries have done it. When such approaches are undertaken, a consultant is often appointed, and a program is undertaken. In the same way, industries chose certain tools & techniques and train their people without any specific goals to achieve. This approach is often referred as "Tool-Holic" approach where the focus is learning the tool and not about organizational development. When someone has a hammer, he will search for nails to hit it! In the same way, once we learn a tool, we become emotionally attached to it.

Lean is a strategic approach unlike other tools & techniques which needs enormous commitments from the management to challenge many traditional paradigms. Often Lean helps to overhaul the entire organization to rediscover itself with a new business model very efficient and effective.

Legacy of Manufacturing system

Before the commencement of 20th century there were no complex products such as automobile or aircraft to be produced in large numbers. Henry Ford started manufacturing automobiles around 1906 based on an organizational model later called "Functional Organization", where the business processes are divided based on its functions such as marketing, design, purchase etc. For example, the shop floor is grouped based on similar processes later called "Process Layout". The key performance measures (KPIs) are decided based on efficiency and limited extent on effectiveness. All industries that came after Ford followed the same model and carried forward the legacy problems. As the time changes, these business models were falling short of meeting the changing customer expectations of quality & lead time for delivery.

When Toyoda, the founder of Toyota Motor Corporation wanted to manufacture motor cars in Japan, he had sent Mr. Taiichi Ohno to USA, to study the car manufacturing systems. Mr. Ohno figured out many opportunities to re-engineer the car manufacturing system which later became TPS – Toyota Production System. In the subsequent chapters you will find more insights on TPS which is later titled as Lean Manufacturing System. In the next chapter, we shall learn the chronological events of Lean as a science.

CHAPTER 2

Genesis of Continuous Improvement (CI)

The concept of continuous improvement (CI) has been there for more than 7 decades right from the time Dr. Edward Deming and Dr. Joseph M Juran visited Japan based on the Emperor of Japan's request to build their nation which was ruined in the Second World War. In fact, these two 'giant thought leaders' transformed many nations paradigms on quality management. They were basically Americans but tired from the resistance of American business leaders during early 50's to adopt CI to remain in the fore front of producing quality products. They were delighted when the Emperor of Japan invited them to share their thoughts for Japan to build their nation. Their revolutionary concepts were against the western world's belief systems during that time. The essence of their teaching to fertile minds of Japan people is as follows:

Left Picture: Dr. Edward Deming; Right Picture: Dr. Joseph M Juran

1. Delight the customers always by meeting & exceeding their expectations.

2. The term 'Quality' is no longer "CONFORMANCE TO SPECIFICATIONS" but "CUSTOMER SATISFACTION"

3. 'Quality' is far beyond the characteristics of the product and extends to total quality that provides customer experience.

4. 'Quality' is not achieved by 'accident', but through systematic efforts of the whole organization.

5. 'Speed of service', 'Zero defects' and 'Total Employee Involvement' (TEI) are the key for attaining leadership positions.

6. 'Quality' is everybody's business and not only the Quality control department.

7. 'Inspection' does not improve quality as it only segregates bad products from good.

8. For delighting the customer needs, the entire value stream of the organization from enquiry to collection needs improvement.

These ideas germinated in the positive minds of the Japanese people who are always ready to change as they know 'Change is the only thing that brings prosperity'. Based on the above inputs the Emperor of Japan requested the Japanese Union of Scientists & Engineers (JUSE) to develop a model for creating a quality movement in Japanese industries and culture at large for CI. The JUSE developed 7 statistical tools of QC and concept of 'Quality Circle' to involve the grass root workers of the industries. These radical ideas were beyond the reach of the Western World which believed in the theory of "Thinkers & Doers" which means only few people in the organization can 'Think'. Later Japan proved the fact that "Everyone can think & improve'.

The regimental job Descriptions (JD) expects the employee to carry out a routine job and he/she is not empowered to think and improve their processes even they wish to. This means that the CI is not a onetime initiative but a major shift in the way people and systems are managed. Japan led the saga of continuous improvement and reached a huge economic growth in 3 decades and then the whole world followed them on CI. This is the genesis of CI.

Evolution of Quality Philosophy

Having seen the Genesis of Continuous Improvement (CI), let us see how the quality philosophy changed over a period of time, which will help us to appreciate Lean principle later. These shift in paradigms are derived from various Quality Guru's thoughts & lessons who contributed over last century. I have expressed the evolution of quality philosophy in my own words here and hence there is no reference is given. The levels indicate the maturity of the organization from low to high:

LEVEL-1: Organization won't last long!

"Sell it and forget it"

LEVEL-2: 'No news is good news attitude'

"Knowing what happened to the customer" is better than merely *"Selling it & forget it"*

LEVEL-3: 'Early stage of Inspection culture'

"Inspecting the product before selling" is better than *"Knowing what happened to the customer"?*

LEVEL-4: 'Process audit culture'

"Inspecting the 'Process" is better than *"Inspecting the products."*

LEVEL-5: 'Early stage of Process control – SPC'

"Controlling the Process" is better than *"Inspecting the process."*

LEVEL-6: 'Six sigma adopters'

"Reducing the variation & then controlling" is better than *"Merely Controlling the process."*

LEVEL-7: 'Early stage of TQM culture'

"Understanding the customer requirements and controlling variation" is better than *"Reducing variations".*

LEVEL-8: 'DFSS Culture' (Design for Six Sigma)

"Building quality in design to produce zero defect product" is better than *"controlling variations."*

LEVEL-9: 'Lean Culture'

"Designing the entire Value stream to deliver customer value consistently" is better than *"Designing 'First Time Right' (FTR) new products."*

LEVEL-10: 'Total Quality culture'

"Setting Quality standard in everything we do and achieving is better than all the above."

The above stages of evolution led to the Business leaders to transform the organization for achieving peak performances. As you could see Lean thinking comes in the highest-level rung of the maturity ladder. Going forward we will see what the rationale of Lean Thinking is before we bring in 'How to implement Lean in your industry?'

Change vs Transformation

When an organization embarks on a CI journey, the top management involvement and commitment is non-negotiable, as what boss wants gets done. The second aspect is the enrollment of the leadership team before tactical level people are engaged. Above all, there must be a business agenda for choosing to 'rock the boat' as CI is not a one-time initiative, as it involves a long-term culture building. Hence, the leadership team need to identify the business KPI's (Key Performance Indicators) they want to target. A transformation approach is challenging the entire performance of the organization that leads to changing the entire value stream from end to end. The choice of tools & technique shall vary depending upon what is the intent of the leadership. Lean is a holistic approach that helps to improve efficiency across all functions of the organization. Going forward we will see how and when a Lean intervention is beneficial. Before deep diving into this topic, a few concepts must be grasped which will help leadership team to make right choices.

Business Objective of CI

Every business leader wishes to enhance the Return on Capital invested (ROCI) for which improving the efficiency of the resources is mandatory. Several studies conducted across many industries shows that the *'actual profit'* earned by the company is much lower than the *'entitlement profit'* anticipated while the business started. The main reason for this is *'Profit leakages'* that occur in the entire value stream which is not accounted in the management accounting systems. In the absence of a system for CI, these profit leakages can never be discovered or arrested. In addition to this, as the organization grows and becomes complex, these profit leakages increase. To identify and recover these 'profit leakages', we need a cost optimization initiatives part of the organizational management systems. Hence, CI is no longer *'Nice to have'* but a must for survival. In the next step we will learn the two types of optimization approaches. Figure 2.1 illustrates the *'profit leakages'* across the entire value stream.

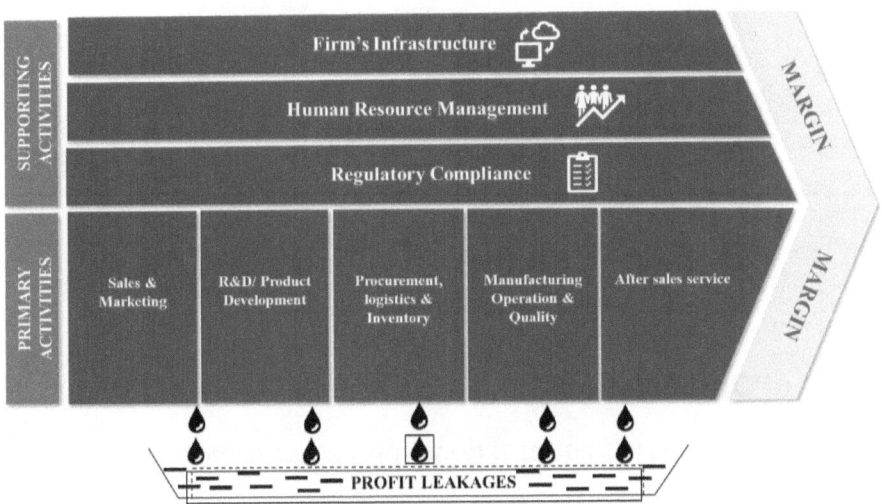

Figure 2.1: 'Profit Leakage'

Optimization Approaches

'OPTIMIZATION' is not 'cost reduction', which could sometimes be detrimental to the sustenance of the organization in the long run. Hence, we need a rational approach to decide what is the right cost for any resources in the organization which is what we call it as 'Optimization'. The following figure illustrates the various avenues where we must optimize the cost. The figure 2.2 illustrates the business objective as "Profit Leadership" and the tree diagram from left to right shows the means to achieve the result till it is drilled down to the granular levels.

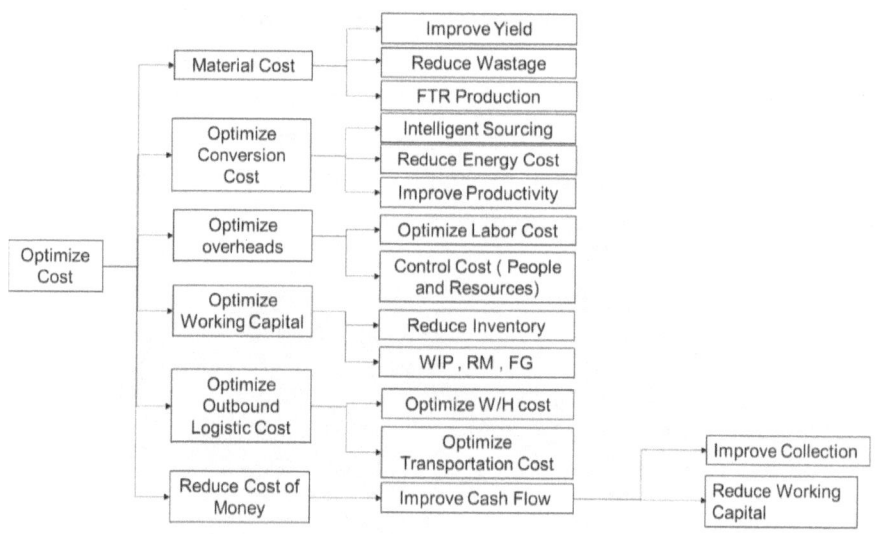

Figure 2.2: Optimization Approach

Types of Optimizations

There are two types of optimizations approaches namely:

1. Point Optimization

2. System Optimization

'POINT OPTIMIZATION' refers to focusing on one process at a time in the value stream taken up for efficiency improvement. For example, if we are manufacturing a crank shaft of an automobile which has many manufacturing processes, we may reduce defects in grinding process alone. This approach is called 'Point Optimization'. Six sigma DMAIC approach is ideal for 'Point Optimization' as it helps to eliminate defects by reducing variations. Figure 2.3 illustrates point optimization of P3 process alone:

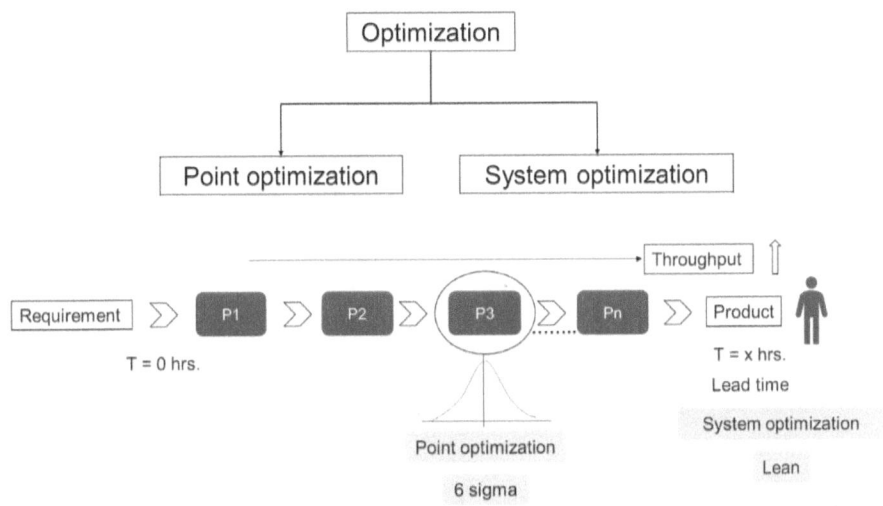

Figure 2.3: Types of Optimizations

'System Optimization' refers to considering the entire process that produce crank shaft from raw material to finished crank shaft for throughput improvements. 'Point Optimization' addresses only the throughput enhancement of one process alone whereas 'System Optimization' increases the throughput of the entire system. Lean is an ideal tool for 'System Optimization' sometimes is also called "SYSTEM'S ENGINEERING" approach.

The term 'Throughput refers to the final output of any system which are first time right'. If we want to achieve the highest level of throughput, we need to eliminate defects at all processes and ensure the material/ information flows without any interruptions. This can be achieved with the application of point & system optimization in addition to DDMRP which helps to decide the right WIP which is called supermarket in Lean (discussed later in Part-2 of this book)

CHAPTER 3

Why to Adopt Lean System?

Before we learn the nitty-gritty of Lean manufacturing system, the top management need to appreciate what is its business benefits. In this section we will evaluate the need for Leaning the organization. The main agenda of every business model is to enhance ROCE – Return on Capital Employed which depends on the profits earned over Capital deployed including working capital. As we have seen before, the organization spends on many 'avoidable costs' due to 'Non-Value-Added activities' (NVA). The main aim of Lean is to identify these NVA's and eliminate them progressively. The approach road map applied for Leaning the system is given below in Fig 3.1:

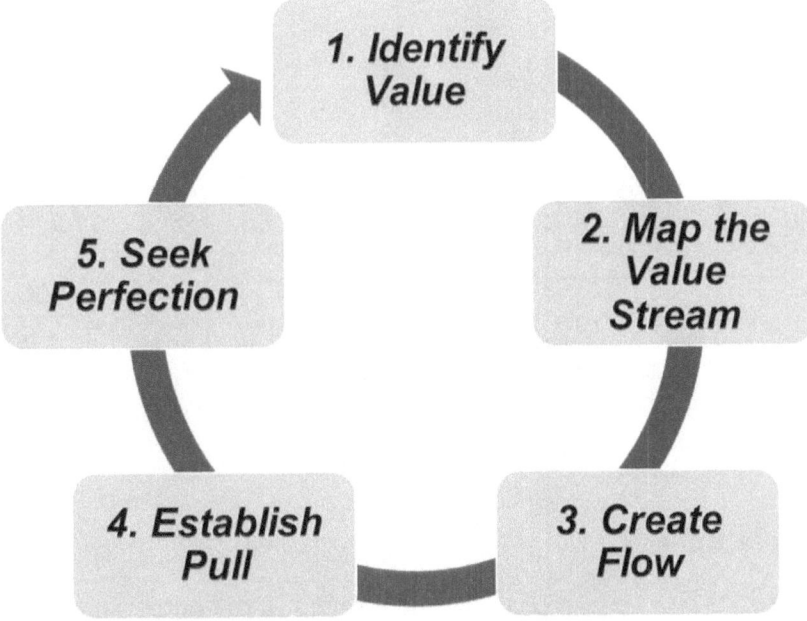

Figure 3.1: Six step approach for Lean transformation

Value Stream Mapping

Often, the CI team wishes to carry out a system Optimization for throughput improvement in the entire business processes from enquiry to delivery, needs to have a big picture of their complex systems. This can be picturized through a mapping technique called 'VALUE STREAM MAPPING' (VSM). As the name implies, VSM depicts the business process flow at high levels showing all hands off from one department to another. Lean thinkers have called it as 'Value Stream' because the customer value delivered through a stream of activities performed by various functions in the organization. The terms 'VALUE' and 'STREAM' are explained in the following sections. A typical value stream mapping is shown in the picture below in Fig 3.2.

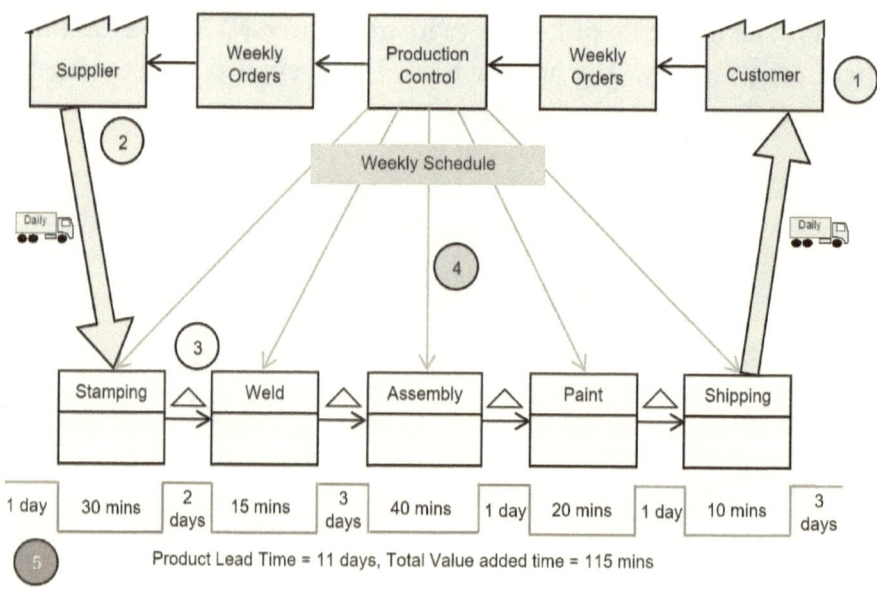

Figure 3.2: Value Stream Mapping

What is 'Value'?

The term 'Value' in the Lean parlance refers to the outcome perceived by the customer after he or she experiences using a product, service, or both. For example, when we are using ATM of a bank, if our job is done within the expected TAT (Turn Around Time) and with zero defects, we feel satisfied with the service although there is no human interface in this case. The same thing applies to a tangible product like a mobile phone or a motor car. Human beings derive satisfaction and perceive *'value for money'* when they invest in any product or service. Depending upon the mode of the product or service, the value may be experienced through one or more of the following categories:

1. Physical – Example: A smell of a perfume or taste of a food.

2. Emotional – Example: The satisfaction derived while seeing a movie or eating in a nice ambience of a restaurant.

3. Intellectual – Example: Learning objectives met after attending a training on vocational skills.

4. Spiritual – Example: Experiencing peace & centering after learning & applying meditation.

The product or service providers must know the value they are delivering before embarking on applying Lean systems. In fact, this is the most important step in transforming the organization. Unfortunately, many organizations have no idea of the value they deliver and spend lots of efforts in their business processes.

Value Stream

We have seen above what 'Value' is, which is external to the organization and the very purpose for which organization exists. Having discovered the 'Value' delivered by the organization, we need to examine how the value is delivered by the cluster of business processes. In fact, the value flows across all functions in the organization right from enquiry received till the payment is collected from the customer. The customer experiences the product or service and perceives a value for money depending upon how the product or service added value to their life. In essence, the business design which includes information flow & material flow across all functions is called 'Value Stream'. As the name implies, value flows across the organization like water flows in a river.

Going forward we will see whether the flow truly happens or not when we apply Lean thinking. Figure 3.3 illustrates the Value stream.

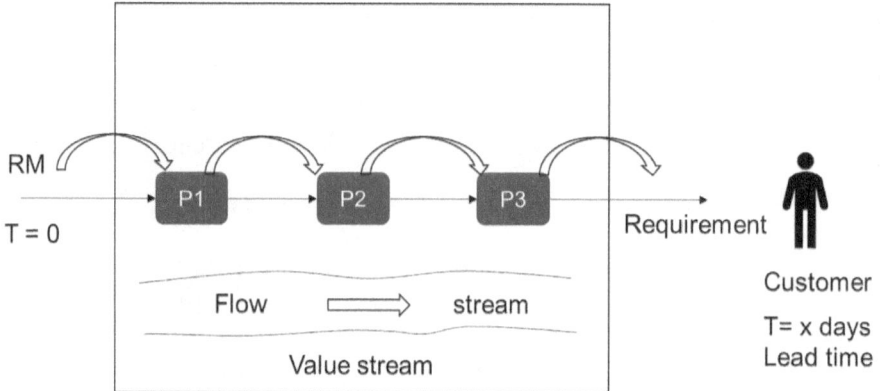

Figure 3.3: Value Stream

'Value for money'

There has been many interpretations and misconceptions about the term *'Value for money'*. Before learning Lean management principles, it is very important to have clarity on 'Value for money'. Let me explain this through a conceptual equation in Fig 3.4:

$$\text{Value for money} = \frac{\text{Utility} \times \text{Convenience}}{\text{Cost}}$$

Figure 3.4: Value for Money

The term *'Utility'* refers to the useful functionality of the product or service. Let us take the example of the earlier land line telephone and compare with the modern smart phone. They are poles apart in terms of functionality. In the land line we can make and receive a call, whereas in a smart phone we can virtually do all our tasks. This is the reason the smart phone has more 'value for money' perception to the consumer. The modern bank services as compared to nationalized bank could be another example for the same concept. The utility of the private banks services has no comparison with the nationalized banks, be it ATM, mobile banking, Google pay, etc. Higher the utility, higher the perceived 'value for money'.

The other aspect of perceived 'value for money' is 'Convenience' which implies how easy it is to use the product or service. Let us compare the telex, fax machine versus internet mails. You will find a sea change in the convenience. Higher the convenience higher the perceived value for money. The cost is in the denominator which shows lesser the cost higher the perceived value for money. From this concept we have learned the following points:

1. To differentiate your product or service, you must strive for enhancing the utility that will delight the customer. The touch screen introduced by Apple is a good example.

2. The designers of the product or service should focus on 'Easiness of using the product or service' which is often referred as 'User Friendly'.

3. To win the customers, the manufacturers or service providers must optimize their value stream to minimize the cost of the product to offer at a competitive price.

From the foregoing insights, Lean aids to re-engineer the business processes to deliver the value for which the customer is willing to pay and eliminate all other activities which consumes resources but does not deliver any value to the customer. These activities are called "Non-Value-added activities – NVA" which will be discussed in details later.

CHAPTER 4

Lean Thinking

The term 'Lean Thinking' is a new paradigm for the business leaders to adopt and transform their organization to achieve peak performance. As we discussed before 'Lean' is a holistic system optimization approach for Re-Engineering the entire business values stream or part by part. Lean principles are equally applicable for both, optimizing 'Information Flow' in support functions and 'Material Flow' in manufacturing. In fact, Lean is a 'Domain agnostic' tool which can be universally applied across any business models. In any paradigm shift there are three aspects are involved as three corners of a triangle as we have seen in Fig 1.1 before which is repeated here for reference.

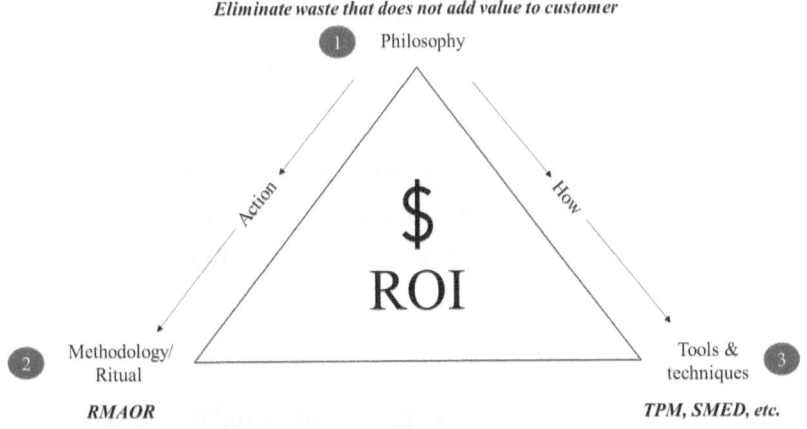

Figure 4.1: Three paradigms of Lean Thinking

The center of the triangle shows the board room intentions to apply Lean principles which is improved 'ROCE – Return on Capital Employed' which is the very purpose the organization exits. The apex of the triangle represents the 'Philosophy' of Lean which believes "Eliminate waste that does not add value to customer". In order to implement a belief, we need a structured approach which is called methodology. Unfortunately, there was no thought leadership to define this as, Lean is a complex system optimization tool. Hence, the author led this need by defining the RMAOR approach which is detailed in this book. The third corner of the triangle is the tools & techniques that are used in Re-Engineering the value stream. In the absence of the three dimensions, Lean cannot be effectively applied. For more knowledge on RMAOR approach please read the PART-2 of this book.

The Toyota Philosophy

The birth of Lean thinking is from Toyota Motor company, an automobile industry in Japan which was later called TPS – Toyota Production System. The foundation of Lean system is based on three principles that are detailed below which are the Japanese words translated in the parenthesis.

1. Muda (Waste)

2. Mura (Variation)

3. Muri (Over burden)

When the Lean thinking was proposed by TPS they believed that these three aspects lead to profit leakages and eroding the value delivered to their customers. Let us see how each one of them consumes cost but does not add value.

Muda: (Waste)

'Muda' refers to the wasteful activity or output for which the customer is not willing to pay. Few examples of Muda are machine breakdown, rejects & rework, long change over time etc.

Mura (Variation)

Any variation causes disruption and panic that leads to defects and waste. Few examples of Mura are scheduling variation, process variation, demand variation, supply variation etc.

Muri (Over Burden)

Muri refers to application of any efforts more than needed leads to waste and hence, cost. Few examples of Muri are excess inventory, producing more than needed, offering features upon which customer does not perceive value etc.

Lean endeavor to eliminate Muda, Mura & Muri.

Laws of Lean

1. Plossl's Law

One of the revealing discoveries is expressed in Plossl's law which states as (Ref to Fig 4.2):

$$\text{Return on Investment} = f \, (\text{Flow velocity})$$

Figure 4.2: Plossl's Law

This means that an organization will earn more profit if it's information and material flow velocity is increased as the term 'Flow' here means the speed and direction of the value stream ability to remove obstructions that will enable faster and accurate processing. Going forward we will see how lean methodology is enhancing flow velocity of the organization.

2. Flow Velocity

Extending the Plossl's law further we find another interesting relationship as detailed below in Fig 4.3:

$$\text{Flow Velocity} = f \left(\frac{1}{\text{Lead Time}} \right)$$

Figure 4.3: Flow Velocity

Lead time is the total time lapsed from the start of the raw material till it is converted into a finished product. The equation shows that the lead time is inversely proportional to velocity which means that the lead time come down when flow velocity increases.

Little Law

In order to appreciate the lean philosophy, we need to understand the Little Law which states:

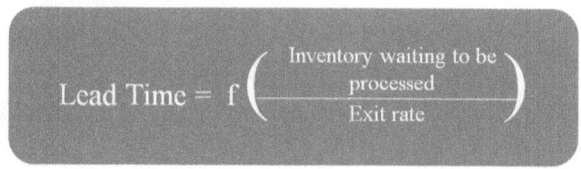

This means that the Lead time will be longer if the WIP (Work In Process) waiting to be processed is higher and inversely proportional to the rate of production of the process. If the WIP is less and processing rate is higher, then the lead time will come down. This law is extensively applied in the Lean system design which we will see later. The following example in Fig 4.4 and Fig 4.5 shall illustrate the Little Law.

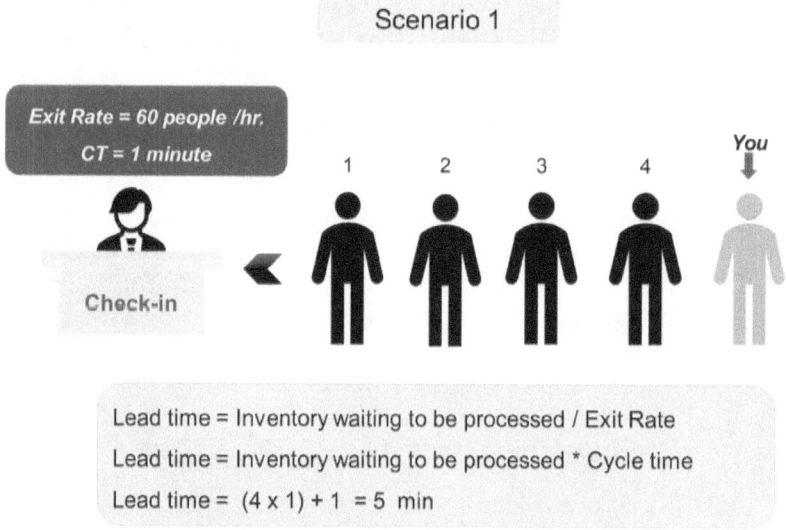

Figure 4.4: Scenario 1, Illustration of Little Law

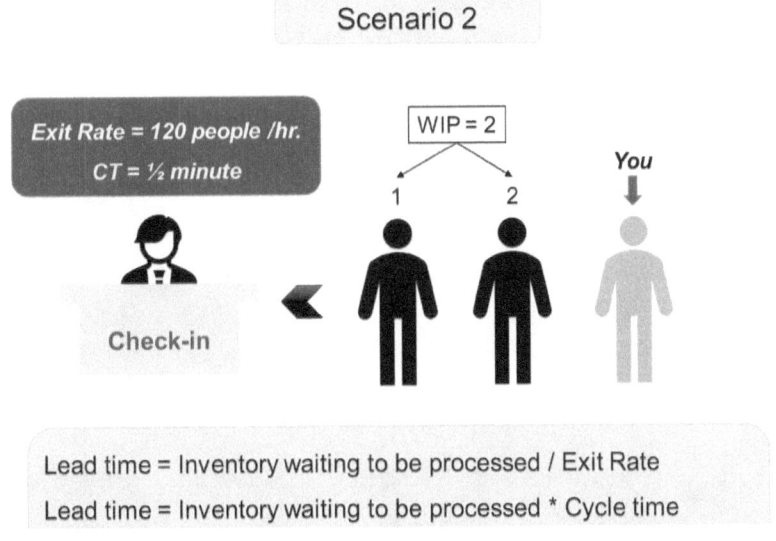

Figure 4.5: Scenario 2, Illustration of Little Law

There are two scenarios of an airport check-in counters are shown, where there are different number of people in the queue which is WIP (Work in process) in this case. In scenario one, there are 4 people waiting and scenario two only two people are waiting. The exit rate in scenario one is 60 pax per hour whereas in scenario two it is improved to 120. Applying Little law to calculate the Lead time to get our boarding card, it takes 5 minutes in scenario one and 1.5 minutes in scenario two. From this incident, it is evident that the lead time is directly proportional to WIP and inversely proportional to exit rate (Rate of production).

Traditional Manufacturing system (PUSH SYSTEM)

For some historical reasons, all manufacturing systems are designed by grouping the machines which belongs to same process. For example, all machining processes are grouped and called machine shop; all sheet metal presses are grouped and called press shop and so on. This idea came from the earliest motor car manufacturing companies from the United States of America which is often called as "Process Layout". The rationale on those days came from the paradigm of process specialization and unit cost reduction. The age-old belief is 'If we produce more the unit cost will be less' as the fixed cost gets divided. A typical process layout is shown below in Fig 4.6.

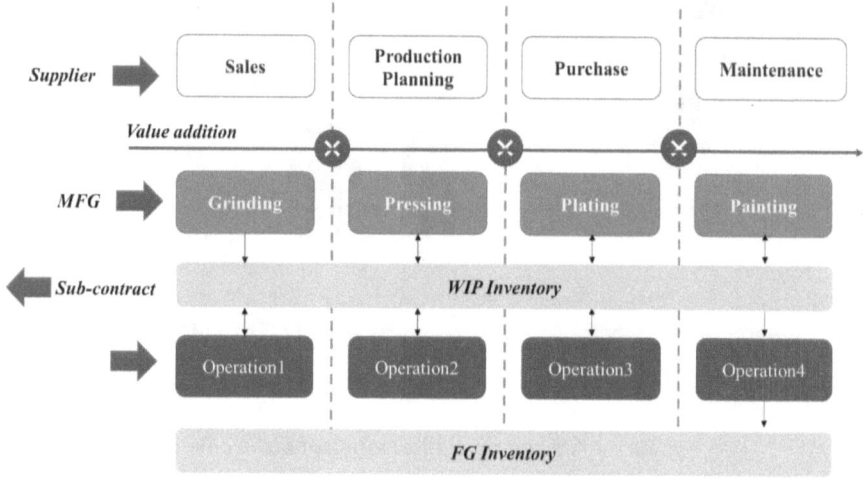

Figure 4.6: A typical process layout

You may also notice that the upstream support functions where information flow happens such as sales, design, purchase, etc, are also created as silos. In this scenario, the major focus is to run the machine to 100% of the time as the efficiency of the plant is measured using the utilization percentage of each resource. This led to over-processing later recognized as "MURI" in the lean philosophy. As we need space to keep the excess inventory these companies created a huge work in process stores which led to inventory carrying cost without any value. Later Lean thinkers called this as "PUSH SYSTEM" as everyone pushes the material out of their premise and derives a sense of productivity. The Lean thinkers realized that unless the finished product is billed to the customer, there is no value in building inventory.

This is a revolutionary paradigm that the traditional people are finding difficult to grapple with. If there is no paradigm shift on these myths, lean does not yield any result as it is a holistic transformation of the entire enterprise. Over the years as these companies grew, the complexity also increased which violated Plossl's law which states the flow only will yield ROI. These process layouts manufacturing system are not capable of delivering flow velocity as it has many flow inhibitors. In the forthcoming chapters, we will see how the Lean transformation applies all these theories. Knowing these fundamentals are very critical to appreciate the lean which is not a tool but a religion.

Lean KPI's

Before we embark on our Lean journey, we need to set our objectives through relevant business KPI's. The Lean KPI's can be classified in the following categories:

Efficiency KPI:

In order to optimize efficiency, we need to consider the following equation where the numerator should increase and denominator should reduce (Ref to Fig 4.7).

$$\text{Efficiency} = \frac{\text{Throughput (FTR Output)}}{\text{M/C + Material + People + Energy}}$$

Figure 4.7: Efficiency KPI

Effectiveness KPI:

The effectiveness KPI's is the measure of meeting the customer needs which decides the growth prospects of the enterprise. The ability of the Value stream is to deliver the 'value for money' perception to the customer as we discussed in the earlier sections. The following KPI's shall indicate the lead and lag indicators of effectiveness.

Lead Indicator:

1. OTIFD – On Time In Full Delivery

2. TBD – Test Bed Rejections (Final Inspection result in First Time Right products or service) measured in six sigma scale.

Lag Indicator:

1. CSI – Customer Satisfaction Index

2. Customer Returns

The difference between lead and lag indicator in Balanced Score Card parlance is, Lag indicator shows the performance after all activities are over whereas Lead indicator shows the potential outcome in advance. The lead indicator is the 'cause' and the lag indicator is the effect.

Lean & system optimization

We have seen before what the difference between point optimization and system optimization is, in addition to how Lean can be applied for system optimization. Through the following illustration in Fig 4.8, I will explain the big picture of how lean helps to improve the vital system performance indicators.

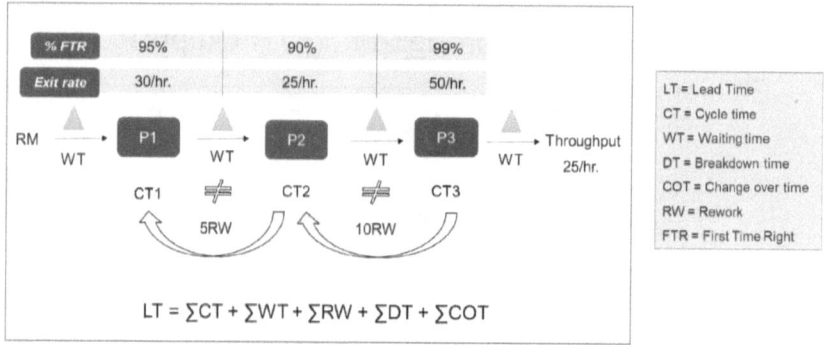

Figure 4.8: Big Picture of How Lean helps to Improve KPIs

Let us consider a very simple system of manufacturing a shaft for a motor which has three operations only, which is denoted as P1, P2 & P3 in the above illustration. The rate of production capacity is given in the figure as:

P1: 30 per hour

P2: 25 per hour

P3: 50 per hour

The First-time right quality of each process capability is expressed in percentage as below:

P1: 95%

P2: 90%

P3: 99%

As the process is not 100% capable to produce there will be some rework at every stage which is denoted as RW in the illustration.

The cycle time of each process is shown in the diagram as CT1, CT2 and CT3 which are not constant as in a real-life scenario. As the cycle times are not constant, there shall be work in process inventory in between each machine which, is denoted as delta symbol.

The most important observation from this analysis is as follows:

1. The throughput (output) will not be more than 25 per hour which is the capacity of the bottle neck process which is P2 in this case. All other outputs of P1 & P3 shall accumulate as work in process. In other words, the capacity of the system is determined by the bottleneck resource.

2. There is a rework loop across all processes as their quality is not 100%. This involves a rework time which is denoted as RW.

3. If any machine breaks down the flow will be stopped or delayed. This is denoted as DT

4. If there is a changeover involved from product A to B, there shall be a changeover time which is denoted as COT

5. The WIP accumulating in between the process shall delay the processing which is denoted as waiting time (WT).

6. If we are to estimate the 'Lead time' for raw material to become a finished product will be the addition of all times as given below:

$$\text{LEAD TIME} = (\Sigma CT + \Sigma\, WT + \Sigma\, RW + \Sigma\, DT + \Sigma\, COT)$$

In the above equation, except cycle time all other times are not adding value as the customer will not be willing to pay for it. Hence, they are called NVA – Non-Valuer Added activities.

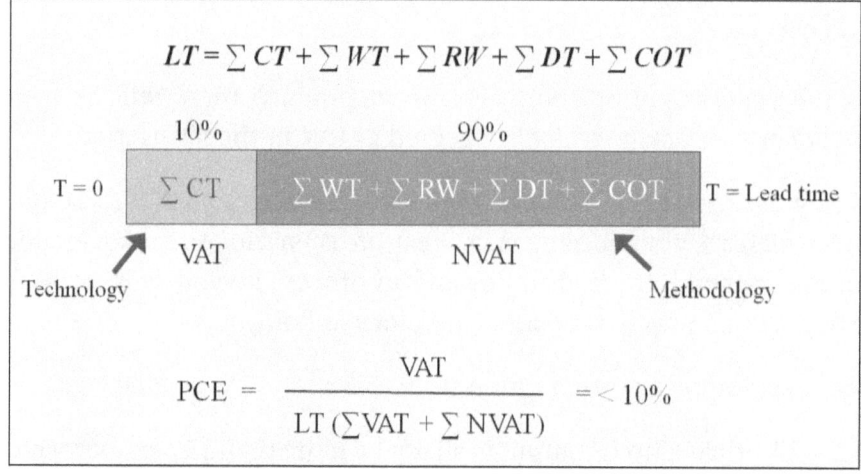

Figure 4.9: Mapping Value and Non-Value services in a Timeline

In the above diagram (Ref to Fig 4.9), the sum of the cycle time is shown as Σ CT and all other NVAs are shown as sum of all NVA times. Most revealing fact of such analysis shows that the Value-added time is only 10% while NVA time is 90%. Hence the biggest opportunity for cost optimization lies in the NVA zone although the VA zone also can be reduced. The most striking revelation of lean study is, the NVA zone improvements can be achieved through 'METHODOLOGY' of creating flow whereas the cycle time reduction needs TECHNOLOGY and hence capital investments. Finally, the metric that shows the system efficacy is called 'PROCESS CYCLE EFFICIENCY' (PCE), which is calculated as a ratio shown below:

Process Cycle efficiency (PCE) = (Value added Time ÷ Lead time) × 100

It is very shocking to note it is generally between 10–20% max.

Hydraulics Analogy

The flow through a pipeline analogy shall make the Lean thinking clear. Just imagine a pipe of cross-sectional area "A" in which the fluid is flowing with a velocity 'V', illustrated in Fig 4.10.

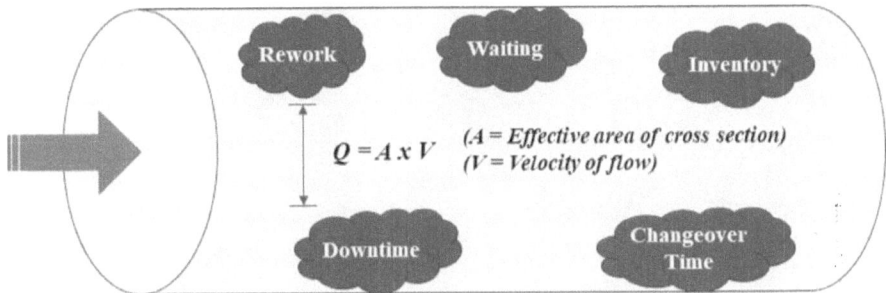

Figure 4.10: Hydraulics Analogy

The Quantity "Q" of fluid flowing in a given time interval is;

Q = A x V

Where V is the velocity of flow.

If we wish to increase the quantity of flow, we need to increase the velocity of flow. In the illustration above, you will find many blockages in the pipeline which reduces the effective area of cross section, with the result the quantity of flow is affected. In our manufacturing scenario, the area of cross section is the manufacturing capacity we have created. The velocity is the material flow across all manufacturing processes. The Quantity of flow is the throughput, and the obstructions are down time, changeover time, production stoppages due to shortages etc. Lean aims to improve the velocity of flow by eliminating the obstructions.

CHAPTER 5

Myths of Lean

There are several misconceptions about Lean and how it is applied. In this chapter, I would like to deal with some of the most important ones to avoid the pitfalls of any organizational development solution.

Lean is a Tool

The terms 'Tool', 'technique', 'methodology and 'ideology' are often used interchangeably for the application of organizational transformations, but it is very important to distinguish them for gaining the benefit of right choices to obtain best results. Let us see the difference between them.

Ideology:

'Ideology' or 'philosophy' in the context of continuous improvement is a 'thought leadership' of a guru who proposed a new paradigm different from the traditional belief. For example, Ford manufacturing system founded in early 1900 was set up on the paradigm of 'Efficiency', which means keep the resources occupied and produce maximum. Based on this belief, all the systems focused on running the machines 100% of the time even if they push their output into the WIP stores as inventory.

The ideology of Lean is "Effectiveness", which means to increase throughput of the company and meet all delivery commitments even if we compromise on efficiency. Lean focuses on "FLOW" whereas, traditional ideology focused on process level efficiency.

Tool & technique:

A 'tool' is a device that helps to perform a specific task. For example, a screw driver helps to drive or remove a screw and cannot be used to cut a wire which can be better accomplished by a cutting plier. In the same way, a tool like Pareto Analysis can be used to find the 80-20 distribution to prioritize a variable and a control chart to find the stability of a process and identify a special cause. These are independent contrivances that cannot be interchangeably applied.

Lean is not a tool as many a times applied, it is an ideology which has its own comprehensive application methodology and tools which is explained in this book.

Methodology:

A 'Methodology' is a structured way of applying an ideology or philosophy, akin to religious rituals are meant for reaching the goals. DMAIC is a methodology, developed for problem solving, applying 'six sigma' ideology – 'zero defect is attainable'. While applying the methodology we may use the tools and techniques such as DOE, FMEA etc. If there is no methodology the tools are useless. It is like the mechanic carrying an excellent tool kit but does not have SOP to diagnose the problem.

Lean as developed by TPS does not have methodology like DMAIC and hence, there are many abuses of LEAN by the practitioners who think 5S is Lean. These fragmented approaches are the result of a lack of methodology. It will become evident that Lean is not a tool but an ideology that applied through a methodology and tools for achieving the financial goals of the enterprise.

Lean is applicable only to Manufacturing systems.

As we have seen so far in this book, Lean is a business optimization approach which can be applied to any business models including trading, contracting, service & manufacturing equally well. Since it came from Toyota car manufacturing plant, people carry an impression that it is applicable only for manufacturing. Lean follows systematic steps as stated below, to discover the waste in the business value stream that consumes cost but adds no value to either customer or the stakeholders.

Step-1: Identify your customers.

Step-2: Discover the value delivered to your customers by your company.

Step-3: Discover and measure the KPI's of 'as is' process and benchmark.

Step-4: Map your value stream of your entire business from enquiry to cash.

Step-5: Identify waste in the system that consumes resources but adds no value to customer or company.

Step-6: Re-engineer business processes that increases the flow of information & material.

Fragmented vs Holistic approach

Most often, a fragmented bottom-up approach is undertaken by hiring a consultant and applying minimal improvements at the shop floor in the name of Lean such as 5 S or Kaizen or TPM etc. This may be a good beginning to enroll and involve the people on the shop floor for continuous improvement culture building but may not give any breakthrough improvements. Assuming, these short-term changes are Lean and complaining later that Lean has not given lasting breakthrough results is futile. These are fragmented approach called point optimization which has no impact on the customer.

Lean is sledgehammer and using it for driving a nail is gross under-utilization of its power. When Lean is applied as a top-down strategy for revamping the organization for achieving a formidable competitive position, it improves the profitability and growth.

'Tool-Holic' syndrome

When there is lack of clarity between what we want to achieve and why, invariably a tool is chosen at random like 5S or TPM and applied across the organization with a fun fair and lots of training and projects. This sets an affinity on tools rather than the purpose for which it is applied. Later, the management realizes that they have given more emphasis on the tools rather than organizational transformation. I heard a Japanese transformation catalyst calling this as a 'Tool-Holic' approach like alcoholic addiction, people get addicted to the tools.

Hence, my recommendations to business leaders and change agents to find out 'What is the end in mind?' and 'Why the transformation is necessary?' before embarking on any organizational interventions. The choice of the ideology, methodology and tools should follow, after answering these questions.

We need quick results and Lean takes long time.

Business leaders often wait for crisis to strike before reacting to the situation, choosing some short-cuts for immediate cost cutting as they feel Lean may take a long time to yield results, they are looking for. On the other hand, the visionary leaders choose right strategies ahead of time and transform the organization with least amount of waste in the system. Among the several Lean transformation initiatives across the globe, Lean yields substantial financial benefits in less than six months if it is applied in a systematic way. The major challenge is of cultural changes rather than technical.

CHAPTER 6

Change Management

In this chapter, we will see how a Lean transformation can be orchestrated successfully resulting in substantial business benefits. The following aspects are key for the breakthrough improvements which are sustainable.

Top Management Commitment

Lean is not a one-time intervention but a long-term cultural shift challenging all old paradigms which needs the commitment of the top management. It starts with the need identification from the envisioning process and long-term environmental changes foreseen by the leader. In variably, the leader has a clear vision of the organization and evaluates its current inadequacies that will be an impediment of reaching where he or she wants to reach in the coming years. Always the vision warrants a strategy which will enable the top management to plan the right approach for transformation. The following steps are followed in Envisioning and Strategy formulations by the professional companies:

Step-1: Discover the purpose of the organization in the socio-economic environment.

Step-2: Discover the Values as the guiding principle of the enterprise

Step-3: Envision the future position of the company locally & globally.

Step-4: Set short- and long-term goals & KPIs.

Step-5: Identify the environmental forces that shall challenge the enterprise in the coming years.

Step-6: Identify the Strength, Weaknesses, Opportunities and Threats of the company.

Step-7: Discover the Strategic Themes that will transform the enterprise.

Step-8: Select Strategic Objectives and Initiatives.

Step-9: Deploy the KPIs at all functional levels.

Case study:

An automobile ancillary manufacturing company that was in a monopoly status in the early '80s has appointed a young and dynamic leader. The company was equally owned by a British company at that time. The organization was doing very well in terms of business share and profitability. However, seeing what is not visible to others is what leadership is all about. The entire organization had the British legacy of process layout and push system with huge inventory and inefficiency. The products were bulkier and more robust more than the space available in modern automobiles. But it did not matter as the vehicles manufactured in India were of old designs. There were no Japanese cars, in cards for manufacturing in India. In normal circumstances, no leader would like to 'rock the boat 'as the company was very profitable in spite of lots of inefficiency.

The CEO felt that the organization will face a serious impediment in the opening economy during which many energy-efficient cars will be manufactured in India. Possessing the knowledge of the Japanese manufacturing systems and JIT concepts, he felt that the company must think and run the business differently. No one in the leadership felt what he is foreseeing is likely to happen. When the leader is envisioning a future and no one else supporting it is an uphill task for the leader to orchestrate his thoughts on transformation. In this case, LEAN THINKING was at the top of the mind of this company's CEO to drive a transformation. Why he chose Lean is simple because at that time all Japanese car manufactures followed TPS in their company. The simplest way to align tier-2 ancillary manufacturers with the OEMs is 'LEAN THINKING'. LEAN became the vehicle of this transformation which made history and benchmark in Indian automobile companies.

Selection of Change Leaders

The transformation CEO needs a team of 'Change Leaders' to realize his/her dream. If the transformation is complex and needs new learning of tools & techniques and people who can learn and adapt to changes quickly are needed. The next step in Change management is selecting a 'Task Force', with a dynamic leader and his team who are known for open-mindedness and conviction to transformation. This is a daunting task in an old enterprise where every leader has a bias over the traditional thinking and way of working. Nevertheless, in every organization, there are very few people who retain their novelty to new ideas and are willing to challenge the status quo. Finding such people is sometimes very difficult as those who have such attitudes may or may not have the right knowledge and skills. Knowledge and skills can be developed but changing paradigms and attitudes are often difficult and hence the CEO often selects a person with lots of passion for creating a new ambiance.

Case Study:

In the case we have discussed above, the CEO had a difficulty in striking a balance between manufacturing technology/system knowledge as well positive attitude and was forced to choose a tradeoff between them. Among his second-line leaders, he could find a commercial director who had the right attitude to lead this transformation although he lacked the technical background which was substituted by another younger manufacturing engineer. Finally, he formed a team of 3 people who will form the task force that will spearhead the Lean transformation.

Knowledge partnership

Lean transformation is a knowledge-intensive intervention that requires an external knowledge partner to train and mentor the task force. Often companies who attempted Lean transformation with limited understanding have failed to bring lasting transformations which is sustainable. 'Seeing is believing' is an adage that reminds us that the mere theory of lean won't help the task force to understand and drive a major change in the organization. The task force must be exposed to Lean manufacturing systems even before they are taken through Lean training in the classroom.

On many occasions, the company chooses consultants who have limited knowledge and experience to apply lean as a major transformation vehicle. In such cases, the company ends up in a 'Tool focused' approach of minor improvements such as kaizen or 5S which never results in breakthrough improvements in performance. Hence, it is very important to select a consulting resource that has rich experience in applying lean as a companywide transformation initiative with proven track records. Some companies have sent the change leaders to Japan and exposed them to companies like Toyota. Even this approach may motivate the team but may not impart any tools & techniques or roadmap for the transformation.

Case study:

The need for a knowledge partner was well recognized by the CEO in our case who selected two knowledge partners one from Europe and one from Japan. An initial scoping and diagnostic study were carried out to visualize the need and resistance to change in addition to quantifying the benefits and time frame. Initially, the executive leadership was trained in Lean to gain their enrollment. The role of the knowledge partner was decided not as a one-time education but to handhold throughout the transformation process.

Resistance to Change

Any change leader knows that people won't readily accept the change as resistance to change is natural. All major changes were not forced as people may defeat the purpose in their own way. Hence, the leaders have limited choice to drive change without the involvement of the people in the enterprise. The following are the primary causes of resistance to change:

1. The urgency and purpose of change is not known to the people at all levels as they perceive 'all is well' as of now.

2. People other than the top management cannot see the emerging future challenges due to inadequate envisioning skills and big picture.

3. People are afraid of losing their importance and position due to unknown future.

4. Unwillingness of people to learn new knowledge and skills that is demanded by the change as they fear of obsolescence.

5. People are not willing to move out of their comfort zone, as status quo although vulnerable, give a sense of stability.

Who offers resistance?

You may be surprised to hear the fact that the maximum resistance is offered from the senior leadership team who are directing the enterprise on the next level to the top management. Their resistance is very subtle and passive which is very difficult to handle for the sponsor. If the strategic level people are not enrolled, the whole transformation will never yield any result. Hence, the first step in engaging the executive leadership is of paramount importance. This is where the knowledge partners play a major role. Often, these strategic leadership people are called 'Champions' of transformation and their education of need and roadmap is very critical which is well covered through a 'Champion workshop' by the consultants.

The next level of resistance comes from the 'Tactical' level people who are in the executive roles in manufacturing and support functions. Their concerns are often different than the strategic level people, such as learning a new skill, fear of losing jobs, etc. This may happen when their roles become obsolete or change significantly. The only way these apprehensions can be removed is through education. One of the Quality gurus from Japan said, "Lean starts with education and ends with education"

Many a time the innocent operators are cited as the maximum resistors of change. In my experience, they are the easiest to change through education and simplifying their efforts in performing their work which Lean is meant for.

Case study:

In the case study, we have been discussing an example of a major transformation of all aspects of the enterprise which makes change management difficult. The CEO recognized the resistance for change and designed a comprehensive education and communication campaign to align all levels of people for supporting the transformation. He invested in a comprehensive training center and modern facility for self-learning as well as hands-on learning of Lean tools & techniques. These investments are justified in managing changes elegantly. There are many strategies that are followed in managing change which is beyond the scope of this book.

CHAPTER 7

Evolution of Lean

In this chapter we shall learn where the genesis of Lean started and tried initially. Although Toyota Motor company gave a comprehensive shape to Lean manufacturing system, many people may not be aware that original thought leadership came from Henry Ford. Although the seed for Lean thinking came from him, it was shaped up as a science by TPS in Japan. Although Toyota created a Lean factory, they have not developed it as a systematic educational package like six sigma by Motorola university. Even the term 'Lean' was coined later in the west to promote this as a powerful transformation vehicle. For many years after Toyota demonstrated economic success through Lean, the pride of the West for thought leadership prevented them from adopting it in their manufacturing companies. This helped Japan to sweep the car market initially and other products across the World helping Japan to become a great economic power. Reluctantly, the west and rest of the automobile and ancillary companies adopted Lean to survive. Even today, the Lean thinking has not reached all other enterprises which remains as a mystery.

The modern manufacturing companies of mass-producing engineering gadgets were not in existence prior to the car manufacturing which started early in 20th century. In fact, the industrial revolution began with the invention of the motor car by Henry Ford in 1906 posing a challenge for building a complex gadget like motor car using people who do not know how to build them. This is evidenced from the quote of the Henry Ford:

"I am going to build motor car using people who do not know how to build them!"

Henry Ford – The founder of Ford Motor Company

'Lean' operating principles began in manufacturing environments and is known by a variety of synonyms; *Lean Manufacturing, Lean Production, Toyota Production System, Single Piece Flow (SPF), etc.*

It is commonly believed that Lean started in Japan (Toyota, specifically), but Henry Ford had been using parts of Lean as early as the 1920's, as evidenced by the following quote:

"One of the most noteworthy accomplishments in keeping the price of Ford products low is the gradual shortening of the production cycle. The longer an article is in the process of manufacture and the more it is moved about, the greater is its ultimate cost."

Henry Ford made this possible by the concept of 'Thinkers & Doers'; few thinkers dividing car manufacturing into an individual processes and developing them in such a way that even a common man can make those parts without knowing how to make them. This was a revolutionary concept on those days which gave a fragmented manufacturing layout called 'Process layout' in which the similar machines were grouped based on the process and were managed by people who specialized on those processes. The process layout manufacturing system is also known as 'Push system' as everyone in the system makes the parts and pushes them to the inventory or work in process (WIP).

Although the Process layout gave the advantage of making the complex product like motor car, it was not very efficient for effective utilization of resources and hence not cost effective. In the early manufacturing system in Ford, the cars were assembled by several people putting the parts together in a single station as the car remaining stationery and people moving.

Before: cars were built in one spot and the workers moved from car to car. This was called the 'gypsy production' system.

This method was quite adequate to make and deliver cars since people were willing to wait for the car and delivery of them itself gave the competitive advantage. Later when the cost became the competitive advantage, the traditional push system failed to make these companies as the lowest cost producers. In order to overcome this, Ford tried the earliest form of Lean by pulling the car with a rope and assembled the parts through operators who were stationary, and this formed the inception of 'Single piece flow' which later developed as 'Lean Manufacturing System' by Toyota. Hence the Lean has born in Ford and later perfected by Toyota.

After: Ford used a big rope and winch to pull the cars along the assembly line and kept the workers stationary

As Japan began to produce motor cars later than US companies, they wanted to build cars which are cost effective to achieve customer loyalty. These efforts brought the new way of designing fuel efficient cars produced in a fast and flexible manufacturing system. This is found possible by making the cars 'Leaner' (less fat!) both in material content as well as with enhanced value!

Taiichi Ohno – Founder of Toyota Production System (TPS)

Lean can be defined as:

A systematic approach to identifying and eliminating waste through continuous improvement, focusing the flow of the product from raw material to finished goods at the pull of the customer in pursuit of perfection.

From the above definition of Lean, it applies to the entire organization which covers the information flow from the customer to material flow from raw material to finished goods till it reaches the customer. Although individual components or building blocks of Lean may be tactical and narrowly focused, we can only achieve maximum effectiveness by using them together and applying them cross-functionally through the entire value chain of an organization.

The benefits of implementing Lean in manufacturing have shown the following results:

1. Lead Time reduced by 20-30%,

2. Productivity increased by 30-50%,

3. Work-In-Process Inventory reduced by 40-50%,

4. Quality improved by 80%,

5. Space Utilization reduced by 30-50%,

Now we are ready to learn how the Lean transformation can be applied systematically using RMAOR methodology which we will see in the Part-2 of this book.

PART – II

METHODOLOGY OF LEAN

CHAPTER 8

RMAOR Overview

What is RMAOR? Recognize – Map & measure – Analyze – Optimize – Repeat

As we discussed in Part-1 of this book, Lean is a major enterprise-wide transformation approach for achieving higher ROIC through systematic improvement of information & material flow velocity by eliminating the waste. Since lean is a system optimization approach, it can be applied in phases to minimize disruption in the normal performance of the enterprise. One of the recommended sequential approaches is as follows:

1. Manufacturing system re-design for improving material flow velocity.

2. Information flow velocity of support functions.

3. Vendor Integration for JIT (Just in Time) supplies

4. S & OP (sales & Operational Planning) process aligning with DDMRP (Demand Driven MRP)

5. Lean NPI (New Product Introduction) process to time to market

6. Aligning Quality Assurance system to 'Maker quality'

7. Re-structuring to suit Lean culture

RMAOR is a systematic lean system design and implementation approach to achieve breakthrough results in optimization of resources through waste elimination which will result in increasing throughput and reduction in cost. RMAOR is explained in greater details below.

R: Recognize

This is the first step in the RMAOR methodology in which the senior management team identifies the strategically important areas/product family where the lean will yield substantial financial gains. Recognize phase uses some of the tools and techniques that will enable the management team to take a fact-based decision. The question that is answered in the Recognize phase of Lean design is:

'What is the most profitable product family we need to apply Lean?'

M: Map & Measure

Map & Measure phase brings clarity in understanding the current process and highlights the waste in the system which can be eliminated in the new Lean Process. In the M phase, the 'as-is process' value stream map is created and populated with the process data. This enables the assessment and measurement of current process cycle efficiency which is the indicator of lean process capability. The as-is value stream map also reveals major opportunities for process optimization.

The question that is answered in Map & Measure phase of Lean design is:

'What is the current process flow & capability and what are the opportunities for waste elimination?'

A: Analyze

The analyze phase of the RMAOR methodology aims to redesign the manufacturing/service system value chain to enable the flow with the least amount of work-in-process (WIP) and optimization of resource. This is achieved by applying lean principles for creating a flexible manufacturing/pull system.

The question that is answered in Analyze phase of Lean design is:

'How can we eliminate waste and create a Pull system with the application of Lean principles?'

O: Optimize

The optimize phase of the RMAOR aims to go in detail of manpower planning, standardizing the work practices, elimination of micro-level waste (non-value-added activities), and simulate the process using software to verify the solutions and assess the risk of the new process.

The question that is answered in Optimize phase of Lean design is:

'How can we optimize the process at activity levels so that Pull system has the least amount of waste?'

R: Repeat

This Repeat phase of the RMAOR aims at institutionalizing the lean system through identification of key performance indicators – KPI's, creation of visual management systems, and establishing a process management system for institutionalizing lean practices.

The question that is answered in the Repeat phase of Lean Design is:

'How can we stick to lean system and institutionalize the practices?'

In summary:

The questions we answer in RMAOR lean methodology is:

Recognize:

What are the business verticals/product lines we must apply lean systems?

Map & Measure:

How good our current process in terms of waste and what are the optimization opportunities?

Analyze:

How can we create a smooth flow in our value chain with minimum waste & work in process?

Optimize:

How can we eliminate waste from our value chain and reduce cost?

Repeat:

How can we stick to lean system and institutionalize the practices?

CHAPTER 9

Recognize

"What is the most profitable product family we need to apply Lean?"

Project Selection:

Unlike six-sigma which is applied for a specific process step for defect elimination through variation reduction, Lean is applied end to end of a value chain, from raw material to finished goods in a manufacturing line, or customer request to service delivery in a service scenario. This approach is essential to eliminate waste and improve speed through the pull system.

E.g.: Manufacture of a motor from raw material to assembly or account opening in a bank.

We shall see various approaches through which we can select right Lean project which will yield substantial benefits to the organization. Project selection is an important step and is applied top-down driven by the top management for best benefits.

Lean aims in improving the competitive position of the product family of any company through:

1. Reducing order-to-delivery lead time which improves delivery commitments.

2. Reducing cost through waste elimination there by aiding the company to offer value for money.

3. Improving quality through defect reduction as Lean exposes defects , faster than the traditional Push system.

An organization may have several product families covering different customer segments earning different revenue and profitability.

Applying Lean in an ad-hoc manner for a less profitable product family may not bring the desired results. Hence the following approach is recommended to help to identify the right choice for Lean project systematically. In the following section we will learn how the Recognize phase unfolds in a systematic way.

Recognize Roadmap (Illustrated in Fig 9.1)

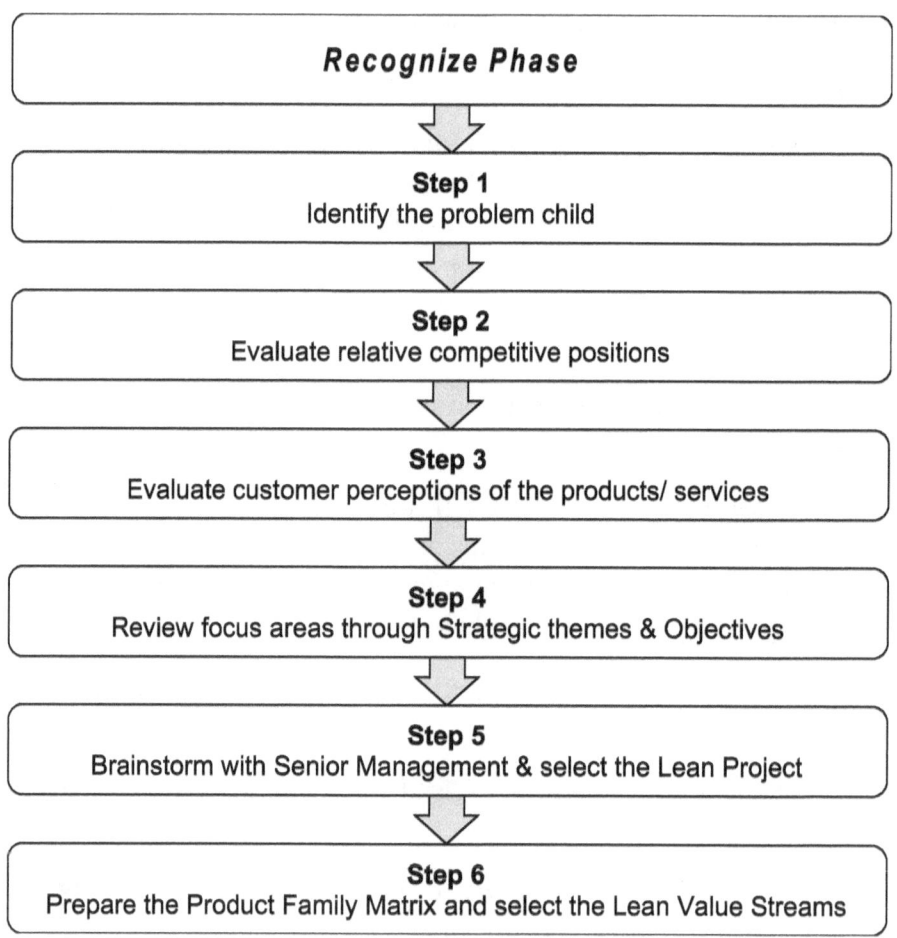

Figure 9.1: Recognize Roadmap

Step 1: Check the business performance to select the product

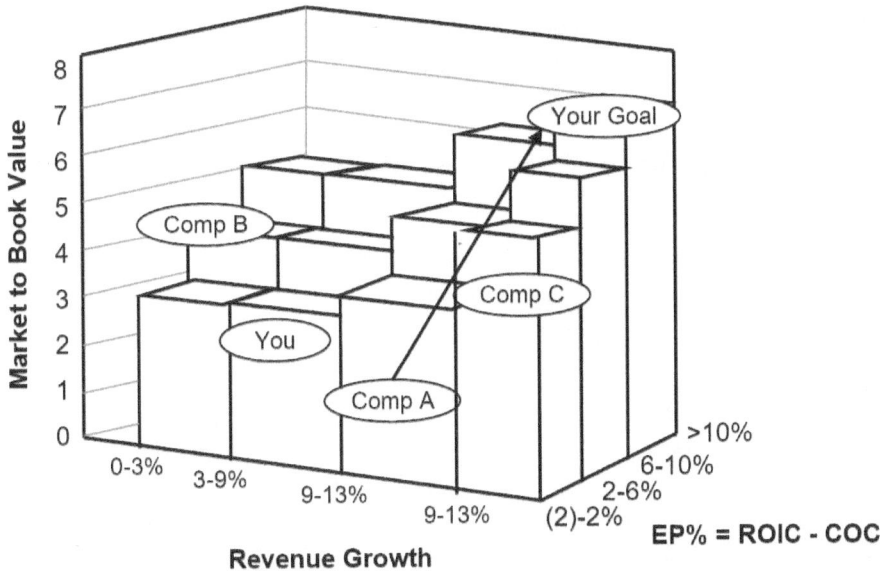

Figure 9.2: Value Mountain

Ref: 'Lean Six Sigma for Service' by Michael L George, Tata McGraw-Hill Edition 2003

First step is to consider the business performance and the scope of the project in current market. Use data available for a single line of business of your own to compare with 'pure play' competitors to know how your company is performing in the marketplace at the broadest level. The most important figure is Economic Profit %. Plot your own figures versus that of your competitors. This allows you to determine at the broadest level, what biggest factors you need to be concerned with in order to drive shareholder value. It allows you to focus on those units that are contributing most to the problem. The reason for the poor performance of the product may be due to poor delivery or low perceived value for money by the customer or poor performance due to defects.

If the current company position is as shown above in Fig 9.2, and its goal is to reach to the top, which project will be the key to success of the company in terms of Economic Profit that will increase the premium that stock market will pay for the net assets (book value) of the company. The product family thus chosen shall be dissected for identifying for improvements through Lean, Six Sigma or Lean Six Sigma.

Step 2: Profitability v/s Competitive position

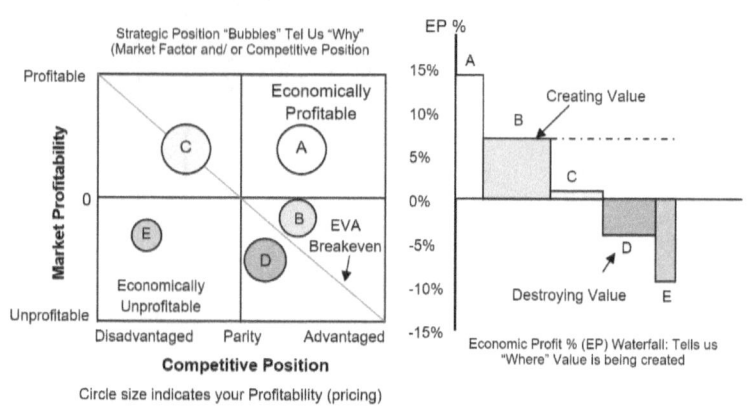

Figure 9.3: Bubble Diagram

Ref: 'Lean Six Sigma for Service' by Michael L George, Tata McGraw-Hill Edition 2003

In the second step, a graph of profitability v/s competitive positioning is plotted as shown above in Fig 9.3. Product A is the market leader with respect to profitability and its competitive positioning. Product B is in highly advantageous competitive position but yields low profitability. Product C is high in profitability but lags in its competitive position. Product D is high in profitability and has fairly advantageous competitive position. Product E is low in profitability and in most disadvantageous competitive position.

Improvements in value streams of product E, D and C would likely to have the best chance of generating significant improvement in ROIC and value.

Step 3: Customer perception analysis

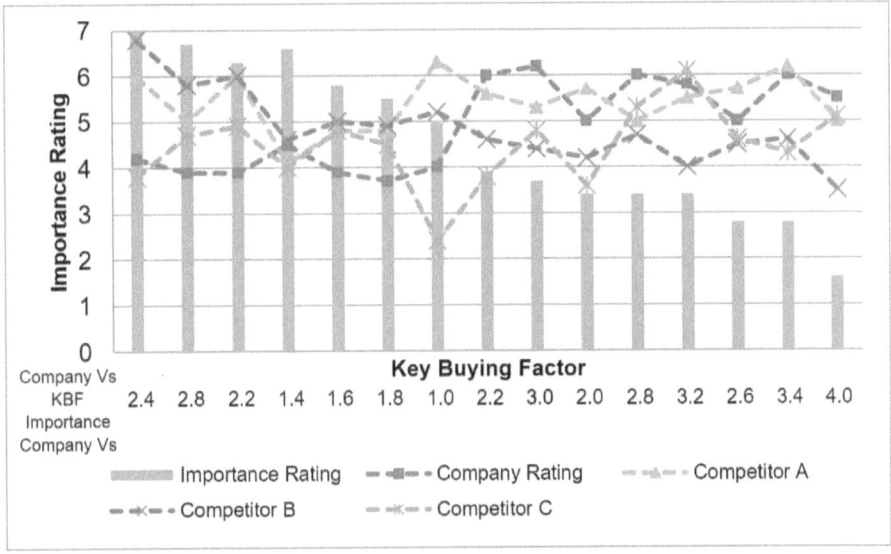

Figure 9.4: Customer Perception Analysis

Ref: 'Lean Six Sigma for Service' by Michael L George, Tata McGraw-Hill Edition 2003

Third step is to consider the project for improvisation as per customer perception. The present scenario of the product is compared to the customer demand or the Key Buying Factors (KBF). The company has to keep a check on its policies that are directly related to the Key Buying Factors. In the above shown diagram (Ref to Fig 9.4) it is seen that the company is falling short of the customer satisfaction in the Key Buying Factors. This company's product is giving more importance to the Key Buying Factors that are least important for the customers and underperforming in the Key Buying Factors that is most desirable by the customers. This company's competitors are doing well in the most important Key Buying Factors as per customer and thus doing well in the market. The company should first consider the important Key Buying Factor as per the customer while improving their products and processes.

Step-4: Strategic Direction

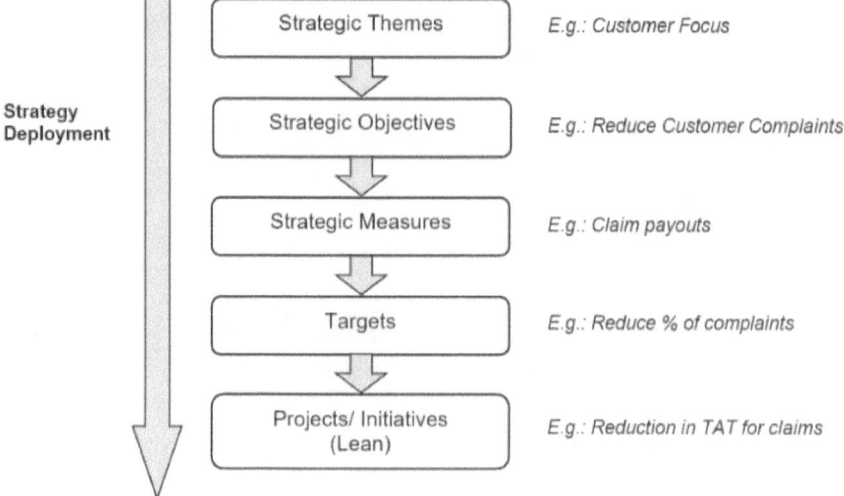

Figure 9.5: Strategic Project Selection

Next step to take a holistic approach to identify a Lean project is to drill down from organization strategy to specify projects. A widely used mechanism to create the linkage is provided by Balanced Scorecard. Balanced Scorecard helps us to articulate strategy by developing objectives in four perspectives i.e., customer, finance, business, and learning and growth. Initiatives chartered against an objective can lead to projects which have a link with organization success. (Ref to fig 9.5)

Step-5: Brainstorming

The last step is brainstorming. The management team brainstorms project ideas that are driving current problems affecting the business. This method creates a list of projects. The team prioritizes the list of projects based on three key criteria,

1. Feasibility

2. Organizational Impact

3. Learning Opportunity

The projects thus identified, can be taken up in the current wave and remaining projects in the next wave.

Step-6: Product Family Matrix

What is a product family?

In any organization many products are manufactured using the same set of processes using the same equipment. The value addition takes place as the raw material flows from process to process till it emerges as finished goods. We call these processes as 'value stream'.

A product family is a group of products that uses similar process steps and equipment within the selected value stream.

Why do we need to identify the Product Family?

In the Lean manufacturing or service system, the processes are sequenced in such a way; the customer pulls material from start to finish. Hence the product family identification becomes important first step in the Lean system design. The Lean manufacturing or service system is designed as streams of Pull systems with common resources in which products of similar processes will be produced.

E.g.: Motors of certain horsepower which have similar manufacturing operations using similar equipment.

How to identify the Product Family?

Product families are identified using the tool referred as 'Product Family Matrix' which is illustrated below in Fig 9.6:

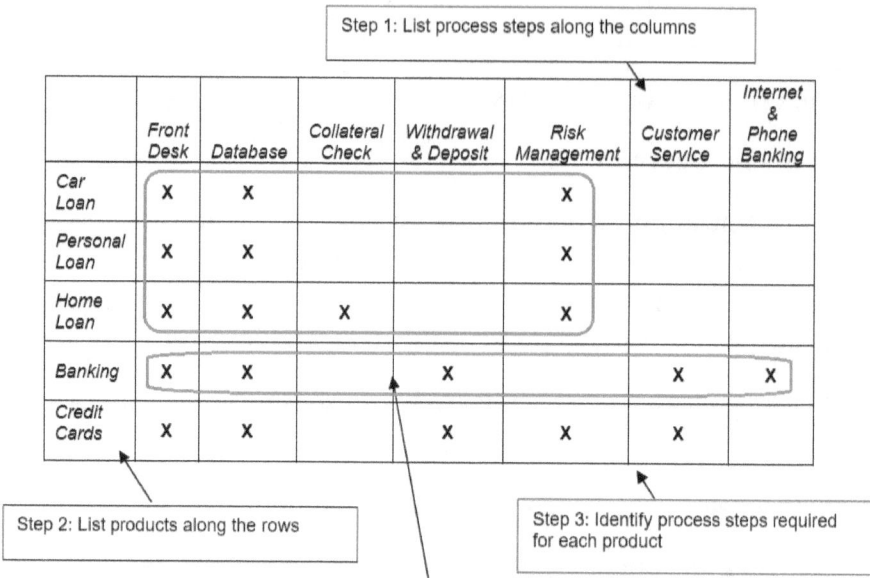

Step 1: List process steps along the columns

	Front Desk	Database	Collateral Check	Withdrawal & Deposit	Risk Management	Customer Service	Internet & Phone Banking
Car Loan	X	X			X		
Personal Loan	X	X			X		
Home Loan	X	X	X		X		
Banking	X	X		X		X	X
Credit Cards	X	X		X	X	X	

Step 2: List products along the rows

Step 3: Identify process steps required for each product

Step 4: Group products that have similar processing steps (at least 80% common steps required to form a product family

Figure 9.6: Product Family Matrix

CHAPTER 10

Map & Measure

"What is the current process flow & capability and what are the opportunities for waste elimination?"

Why Map & Measure?

Analyzing a value stream to eliminate waste requires clear understanding of how the current system works and where the waste is hidden. In the Six Sigma methodology the Define phase is intended to bring clarity of the real-life problem where the current data is collected to see the magnitude and impact of the problem upon the business. Similarly in Lean, map & measure step brings clarity of the scope of the problem and the team understands problem in an identical manner.

The map & Measure phase has several steps to bring clarity about the current condition of the business value stream which will facilitate easy analysis of waste that consumes resources but does not add any value to the customer or for the organization. The following figure 10.1 illustrates these mapping techniques and subsequent measures that will establish the baseline efficiency of our value stream.

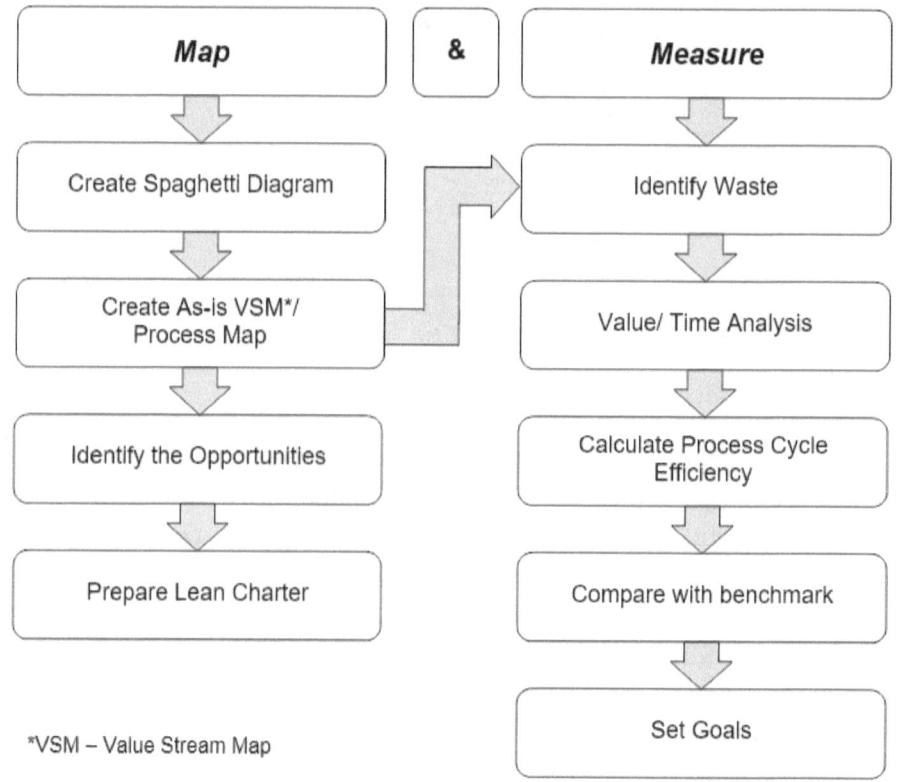

Figure10.1: Map & Measure Roadmap

Mapping the process

Mapping the value stream is carried out using the following tools. Each tool has the power of highlighting the problem in the current manufacturing or service system.

1. Spaghetti Diagram – To show the physical flow of material or information.

2. CVSM (Current state Value stream map) – To show the high-level process flow from raw material to finished goods including the process data.

3. Process Maps – To show the activities at the granularity levels to examine their value addition.

Spaghetti Diagram

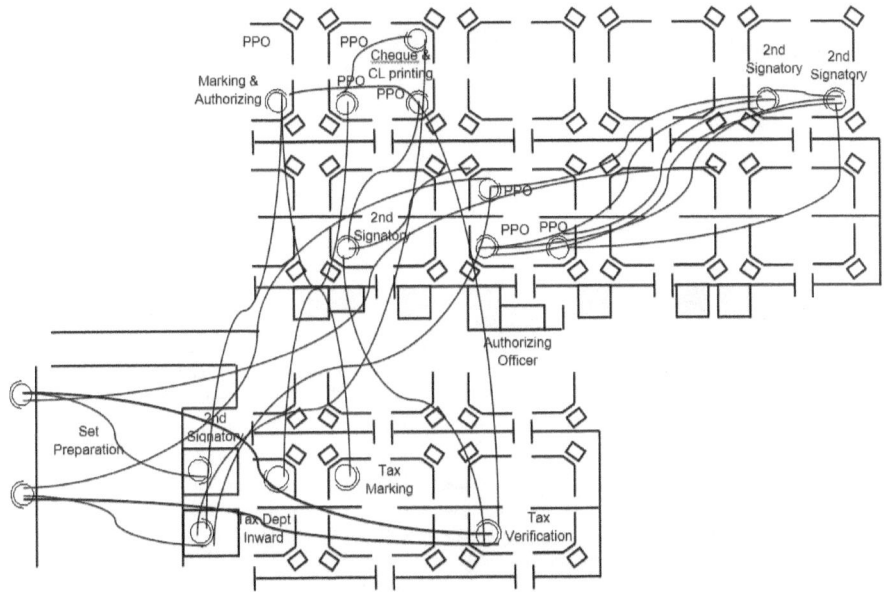

Figure 10.2: Spaghetti Diagram

The traditional manufacturing and service processes are often carried out in batch processing where the material or information's flow from one part of the factory to another generally in a jumbled-up manner. Tracking the path of material commencing from raw material to finished goods in actual physical factory layout gives a picture of excessive movements and validates the Product family groupings that use common equipment and processes. A typical Spaghetti diagram is shown above in Fig. 10.2.

Current state VSM

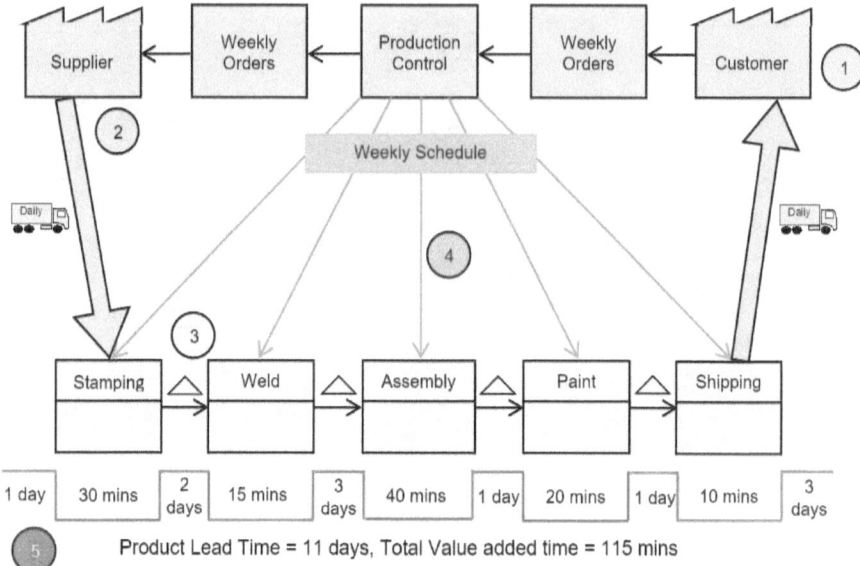

Figure 10.3: Current state Value Stream Map

Value Stream Map is a visual representation of the flow (Ref to Fig 10.3)

1. Includes every step in the process Value Added – VA and Non-Value-Added – NVA.

2. Includes both the material and the information flows.

3. Covers the entire value stream within the facility or Product Family

Why use a VSM?

1. To work on the bigger picture, not just individual processes.

2. To improve the whole, not just to optimize the parts.

3. To include both information and material flow.

4. Pictures are worth a thousand words.

5. But it is not just to draw a picture, it is to understand entire process

The VSM can be created by paper and pencil or using software like iGrafx®. While using the software the standard icons pop up and offer a template making it easier to construct. While preparing using paper & pencil use the following standard icons. The VSM is constructed using standardized icons which represents any activity that consumes resources for delivering value to internal or external customers. In the following page, you will learn these symbols and their meaning (Ref to Fig 10.4A and 10.4B).

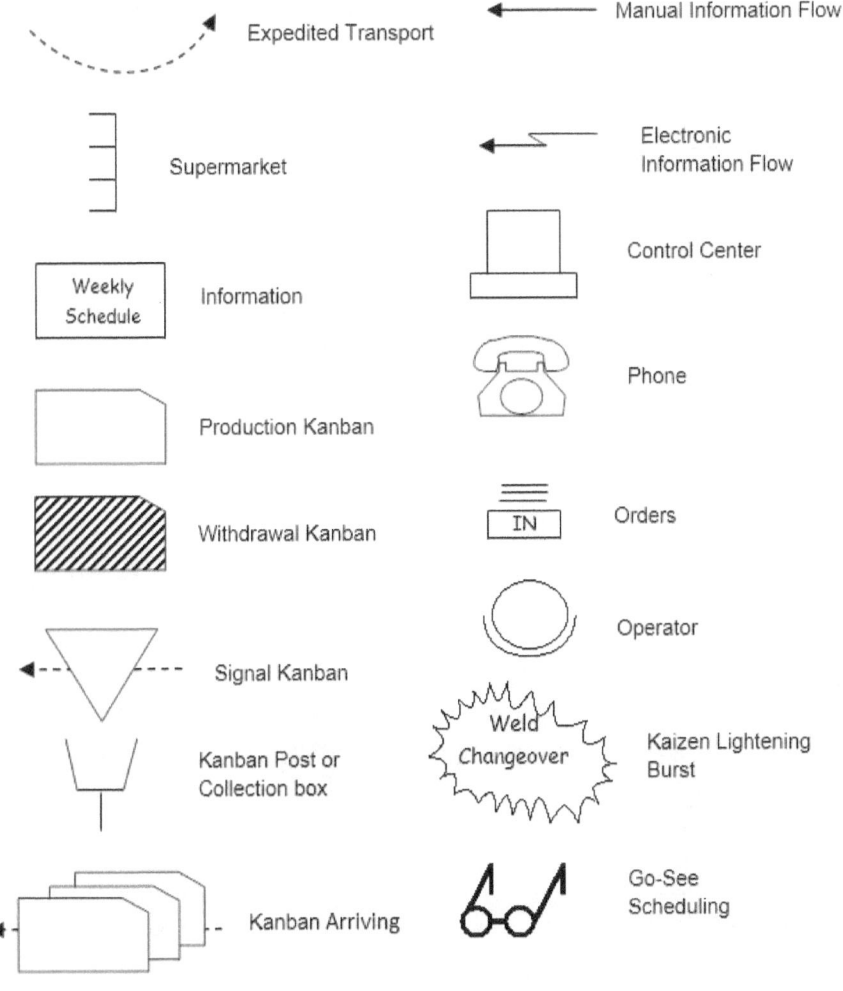

Figure 10.4A: VSM Icons

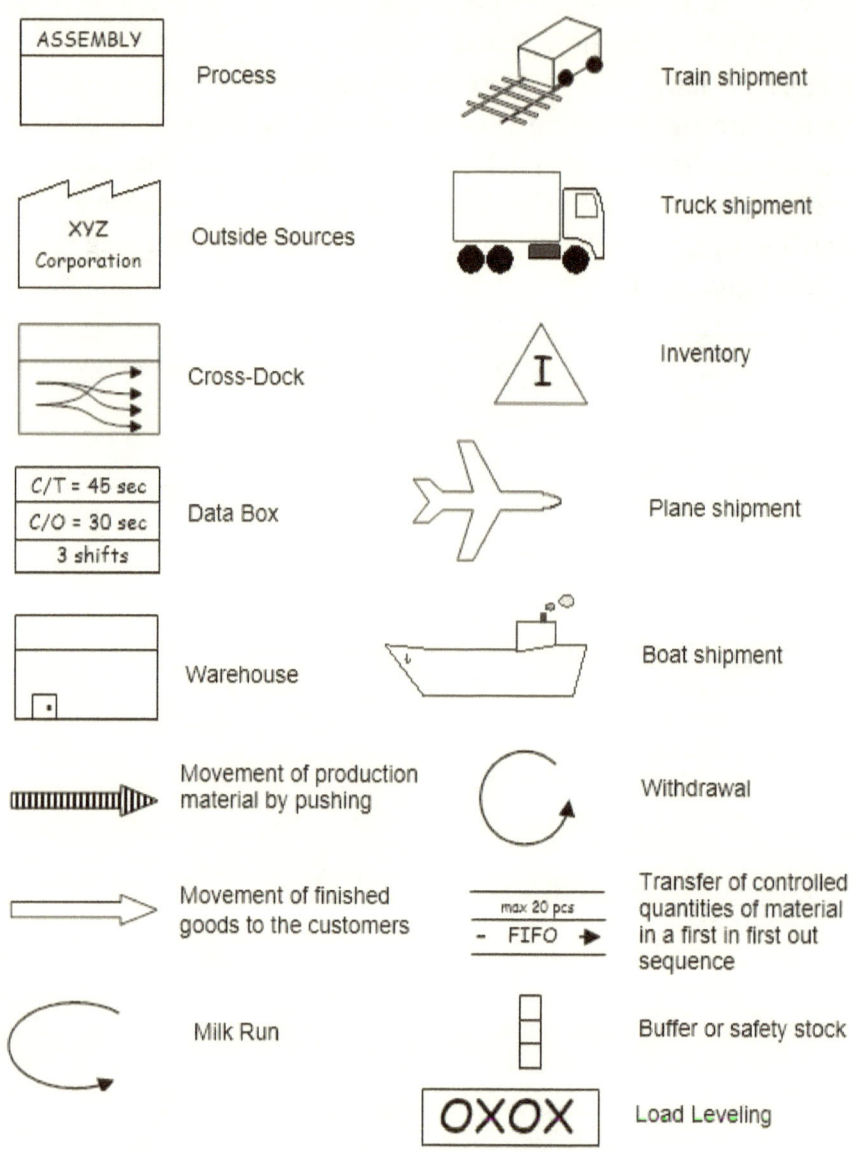

Figure 10.4B: VSM Icons

Steps for constructing VSM

1. Map customer requirement information.

2. Map order information flows.

3. Map physical product/material flows.

4. Add process data.

5. Summarize current state.

6. Identify the areas of improvement.

These steps are detailed in the following sections

Step-1: Map customer requirements:

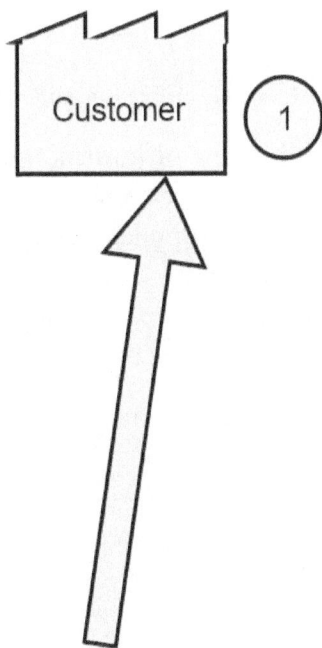

Figure 10.5: Map customer requirements

Capture the following data from the customer (ref to Fig 10.5):

1. Delivery requirements including quantities, mix, batch size, seasonality, etc.

2. Delivery frequency – quantity per day or week etc.

Step-2: Map order information flow

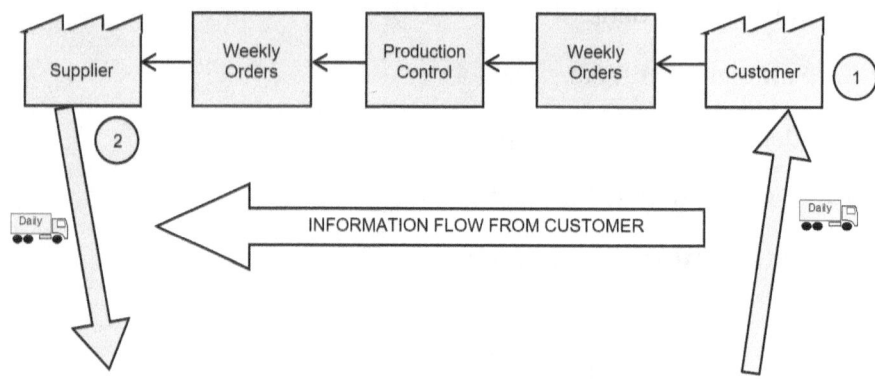

Figure 10.6: Map order information flow

In this step, we capture the flow of information from customers into the organizational functions which converts them into actions to produce the product right from suppliers from the inbound logistics to the arrival of material into the stores. In the service delivery scenario, it tracks the flow of information from customer request to service delivery. Please refer the Fig 10.6 for details.

Step-3: Map physical product/material flows

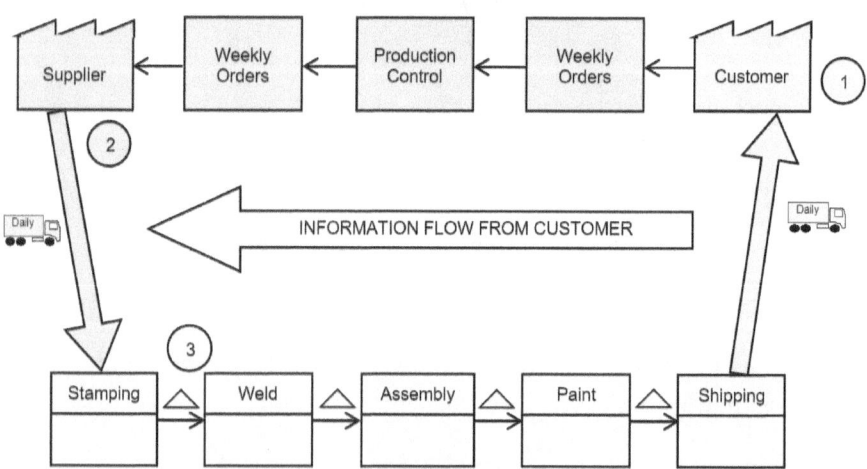

Figure 10.7: Map physical product/material flows

In this step, we track the high-level process steps which convert raw material into value added finished goods in a manufacturing company and customer request into a service delivery in a service company. Caution to be exercised not to capture activities at the granular level but to capture process steps that convert a raw material into a finished good. The picture shows an example where process names are entered into the process boxes at the bottom of the VSM. (Ref to Fig 10.7)

Step-4: Add process Data

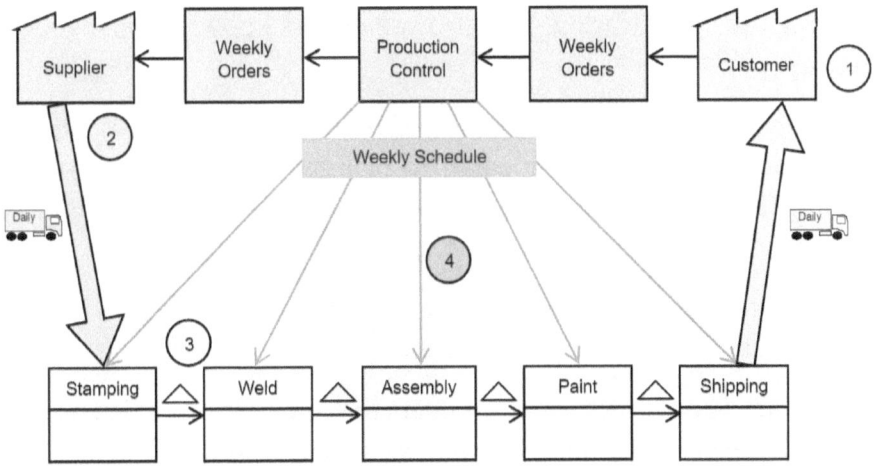

Figure 10.8: Add process Data

In this step all relevant process data is collected to get an insight of the value stream and subsequently calculate the process cycle efficiency. The data analysis also helps to identify the improvement opportunities. (Ref to Fig 10.8)

The desirable process data collected are detailed below:

Lead Time (LT): It is the total lapsed time from the time raw material starts its journey and the time it gets converted as finished goods. It is the sum of process time and waiting time between processes.

Cycle Time (CT): It is time taken for the product to go through a single process in the value stream. CT indicates the rate measure and not the lapsed time in a process. As the name implies a 'cycle' refers when the operator picks up the product and places it after the process and picks up the next.

Setup Time (ST): ST is the elapsed time between the last produced part of the previous batch to the normal production is started for the changeover part in a process. For example, in a plastic moulding process, it is the time between the changeover from one mould to another. It comprises of unloading & loading of the tool, setting up the equipment parameters and taking trials till the new part is meeting the specification. It is also sometimes known as changeover time.

Up Time (UT): It is the percentage of time the equipment is capable of running the process compared to planned time available for the process. This measure gives an idea on the effectiveness of maintenance process.

Rework rate: It is the percentage of products that must be reworked to meet the specification in any process step.

Scrap Rate: The percentage of products that must be discarded as they cannot be reworked to make them meet specification.

Number of Operators: The number of people deployed in a process step. If the person works part time, it can be expressed as a fractional or decimal number.

Available Time (AT): It is the time available in a given shift or day during which the value stream can operate if there is a customer demand. It is often calculated deducting the breaks from the shift time.

Inventory: It is the number of units waiting to be processed in between two processes. In VSM, it is denoted by a delta symbol with the unit numbers written inside the symbol. Greater is the number of inventories, it indicates that the process ahead is a bottle neck.

Step-5: Summarize current state

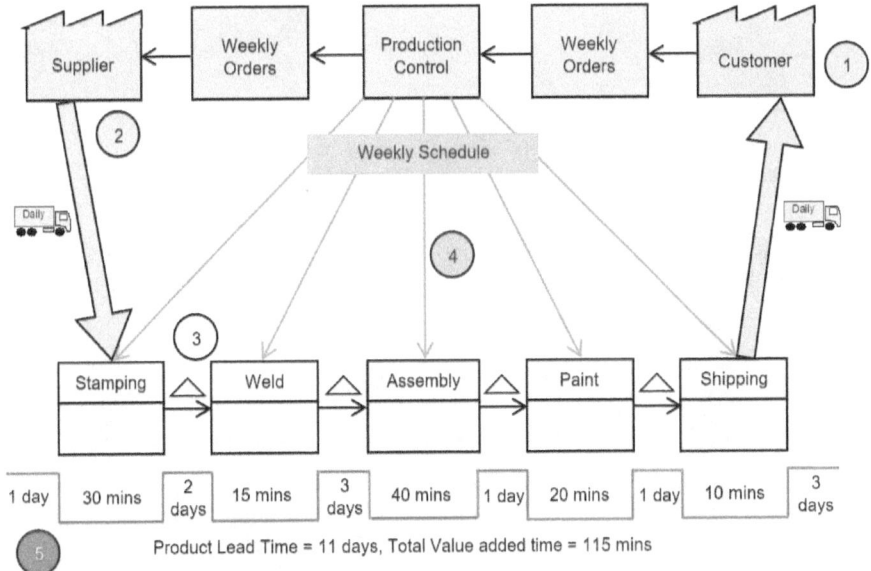

Figure 10.9: Summarize current state

In this step we compute the following time measures:

1. Product Lead time = Sum of all processing time + waiting time in between process steps.

2. Value added time = sum of all processing time alone. (Ref to Fig 10.9)

Note: Here we assume that all process time is value adding.

Step-6: Identify areas of improvement

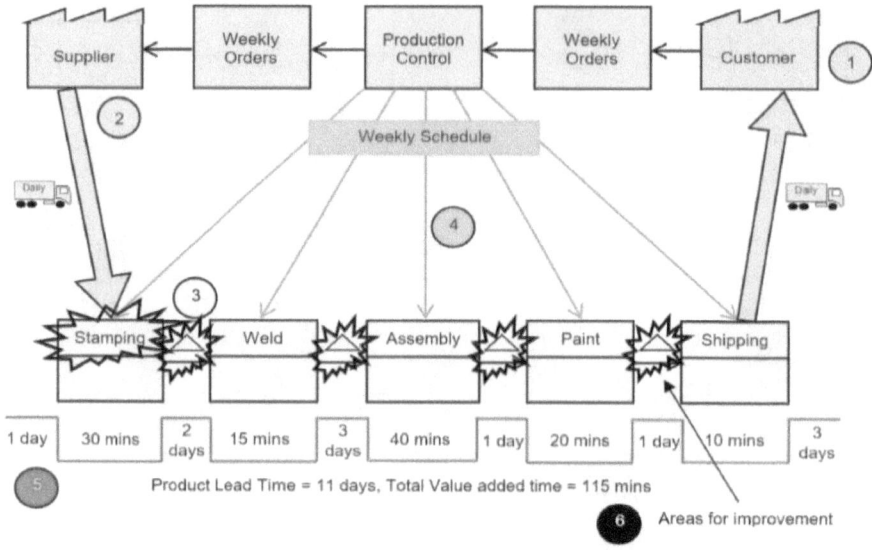

Figure 10.10: Identify areas of improvement

In this step we identify the area for improvements based on high work in process inventory (WIP) and high lead time for the processes in relevance to the downtime of the machines or unavailability of operators (Ref to Fig 10.10).

Process Mapping

Many occasions in addition to VSM, we may have to represent the processes in more granular levels of some of the major process steps in the VSM. In service processes sometimes it may be sufficient to map processes using process maps instead of VSM particularly when the area of improvement is local rather than end to end. In the above situations, we can use process maps of the following types:

SIPOC (Supplier-Input-Process-Output-Customer)

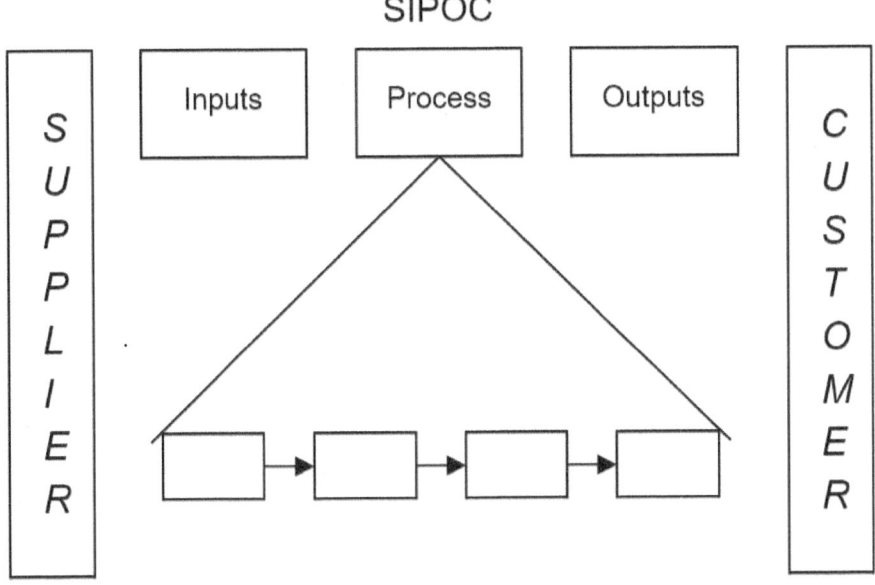

Figure 10.11: SIPOC

SIPOC is generally used for representing macro level process steps that shows the scope of project under study (Ref to Fig 10.11). It is one of the tools used in DMAIC.

Activity Process Maps

Activity Process maps as the name implies, shows what happens in the process at activity levels using the standard symbols (Ref to Fig 10.12).

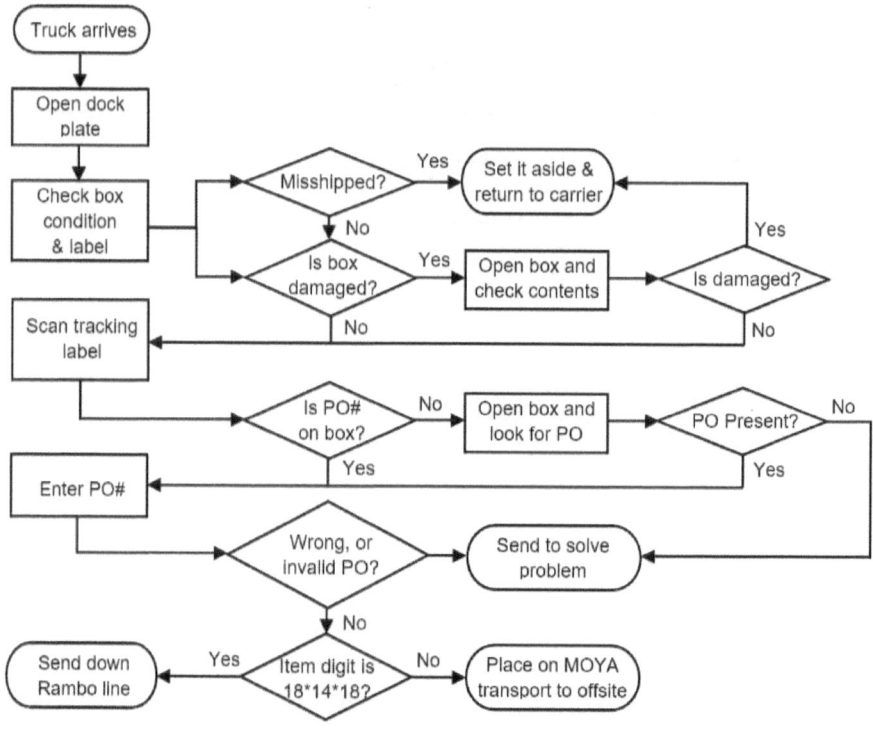

Figure 10.12: Activity Process Map

Deployment Process Maps:

Deployment process maps in addition to activities shows the functions in which they are performed clearly indicating the hands-off (Ref to Fig 10.13).

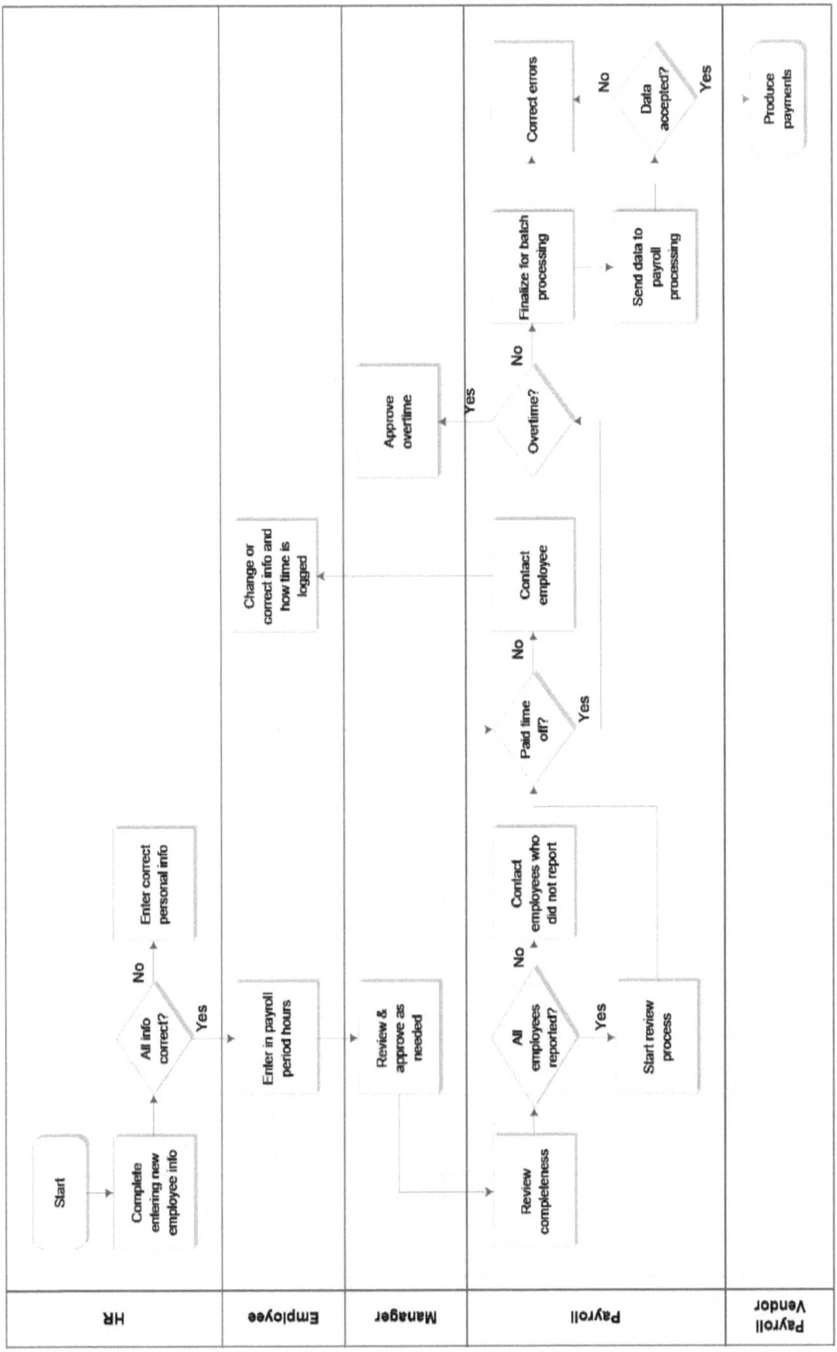

Figure 10.13: Deployment Process Flowchart

Create Lean Charter

Having mapped the current state value stream map, we have enough information to define the problem through the Lean charter which can be presented to steering committee for approval in the Toll gate review. This marks the completion of the Mapping part of this phase in the RMAOR methodology.

A typical charter format is given below in Fig 10.14:

Lean Project Charter						
What			Description of Process			
Process		Description of Process & Problem Statement				
Station Manager		Goal				
Process Owner/ Team Leader		Product Family				
Approval Date		Available timestamps/ process parameters				
Dependencies		In-scope		Out of Scope		
Risks		Productivity View		Process Lead Time/ Cycle Time		
				Average		
Impact on Business		Productivity KPI		Standard Deviation		
		Other Productivity KPI		Customer Expectation		
Business Case				Target		

Figure 10.14: Lean Project Charter Format

Measure

In the previous sections, we have seen how to represent the as-is process using Current state VSM or Process maps. Now in this section, we shall see how the baseline process capability of a process is calculated.

Let's detail the above steps in the measure phase in Fig 10.15:

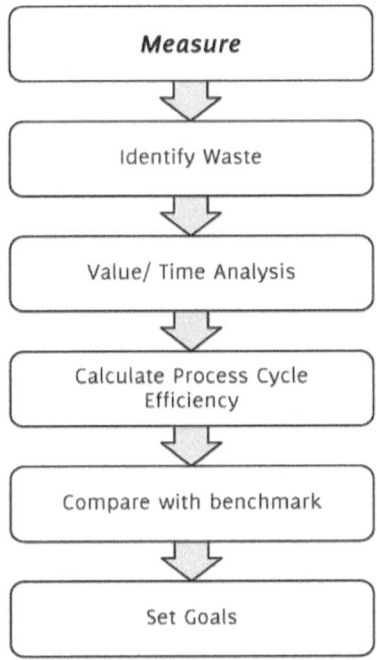

Figure 10.15: Measure Roadmap

Identify Waste

Lean manufacturing or service system aims to eliminate the 7 sins of waste often called by the acronym TIMWOOD from the first letter of these wastes:

T – Waste of Transportation

I – Waste of Inventory

M – Waste of Motion

W – Waste of Waiting

O – Waste of Overproduction

O – Waste of Overprocessing

D – Waste of Defects

Waste of Transportation – T

Waste of materials, parts, assembled goods or files, emails, information (service) when they are transported/transferred from one workstation to the other during the processing.

Waste of Inventory – I

Waste of materials, parts, assembled goods (manufacturing) or files, emails, information (service) when they are purchased, produced, or delivered in advance of when the customer needs them.

Waste of Motion – M

Waste caused by non-value-added movement of operators and production machines.

Waste of Waiting – W

Waste caused by not having all the material, parts, supplies or information available exactly when needed for the operator to do their value-added job without interruption.

Waste of Overproduction – O

Waste caused by producing more than consumers buy. This type of waste leads to excessive inventories.

Waste of Over processing – O

Waste of unnecessary processes and operations.

Waste of Defects – D

Waste that occurs when a product does not conform to proper specifications i.e., defect. The result could involve product rework or scrap.

The above wastes are identified in the Process maps so that they can be challenged for elimination in the analyze phase.

Time & Value Analysis

Value Analysis (Ref to fig 10.16)

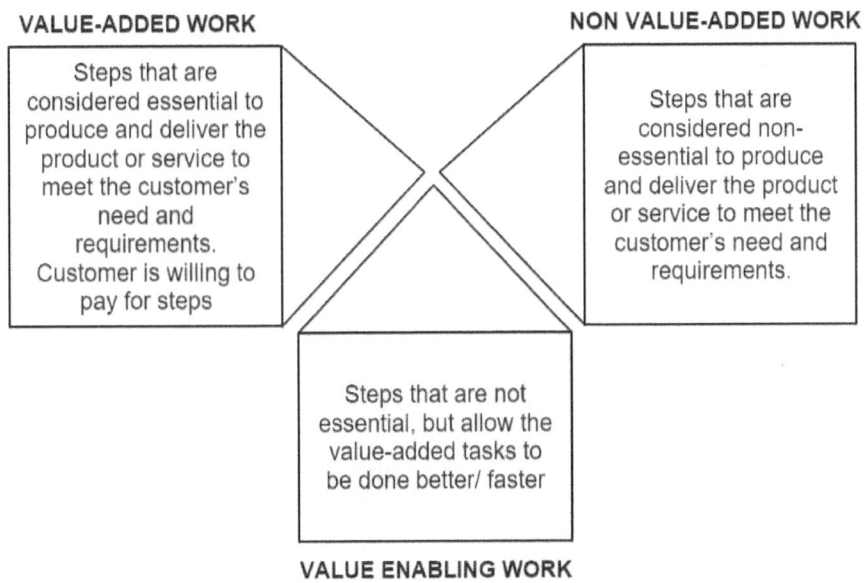

Figure 10.16: Classification of activities

Value adding activity (VA):

The value adding activity is the activity that physically changes the product there by adding value for which the customer is willing to pay.

Non-value adding activity (NVA):

Non-value-added activity is essentially the waste described in the previous section for which the customer is not willing to pay.

Business Value adding or Value enabling activity (BVA):

BVA are those activities business needs but not by the customer such as legal, finance management, training etc. Using the above classification all the activities in the Process maps are classified as VA, BVA and NVA. This step is known as Value analysis.

Time Analysis

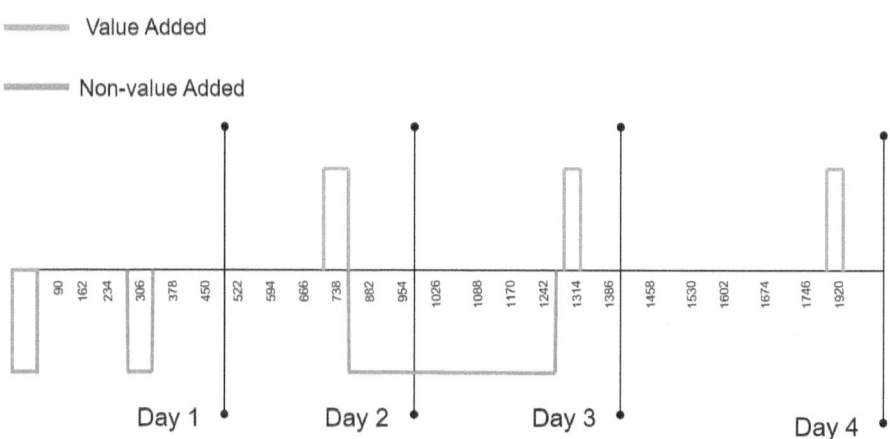

Figure 10.17: Time Value Map

In this step, we collect time data of various activities (value-added and non-value added) and map it in a time value map shown above in Fig 10.17. In the above illustration, the activities shown below the line are the NVAs, the ones shown above the line are the value-added activities. The time axis is shown in minutes and the width of the bar indicates the duration.

Calculate Process Cycle Efficiency

The next step in Measure is Time analysis and calculation of Process cycle efficiency which is given by the equation:

Process Cycle Efficiency = (Value added time ÷ Lead time) X 100 %

The value-added time in VSM is the sum of processing time whereas, if process mapping is used, then all VA activity time should be summed up for Value-added time. The total time is nothing but VA time + NVA time.

The Process Cycle Efficiency indicates the opportunity for eliminating NVAs and often calculated after the process is improved in analyze phase.

Compare with Benchmark & Set Goals

After computing the current state Process cycle efficiency, the next step is to aim at the world class benchmarks and set a goal for Lean system to be designed. Typical process cycle efficiency in various types of World class industries is given below in Fig 10.18:

Application	Typical cycle efficiency (Batch Processing)	World-class cycle efficiency (Lean)
Continuous Manufacturing	5%	30%
Business processes – Service	10%	50%
Business processes (Creative/Cognitive)	5%	25%

Figure 10.18: World class benchmark

CHAPTER 11

Analyze

Why to analyze the VSM?

The CVSM created in the previous step along with process maps depicts the as-is process flow along with NVAs and waste such as high inventory, down times, rejects & rework etc. The analyze phase is intended to:

1. Identify the opportunities for improvements.

2. Create the Pull system using the Future state VSM.

Analyze Roadmap (Illustrated in Fig 11.1):

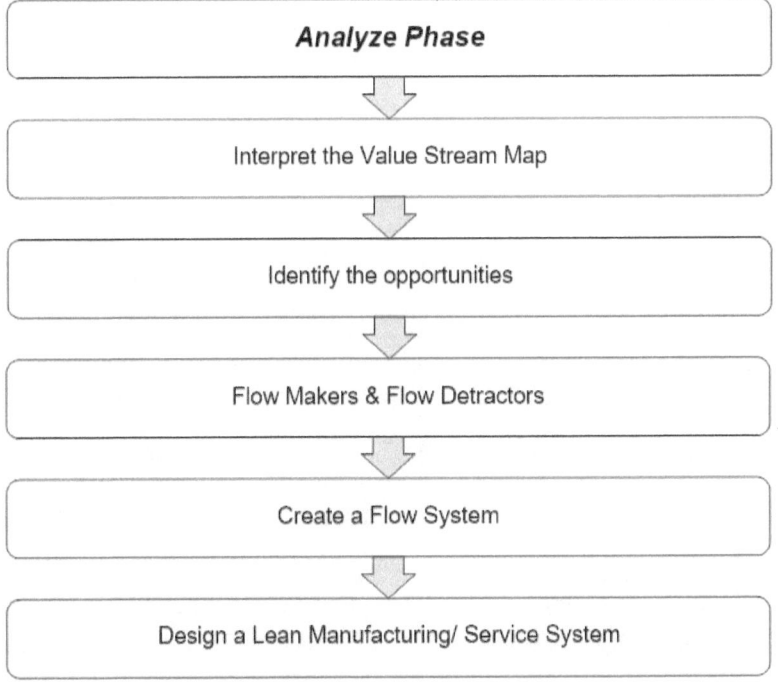

Figure 11.1: Analyze Roadmap

Interpret the CVSM

Inspecting the current state VSM and process maps we can identify the waste in the manufacturing/service system which is explained below:

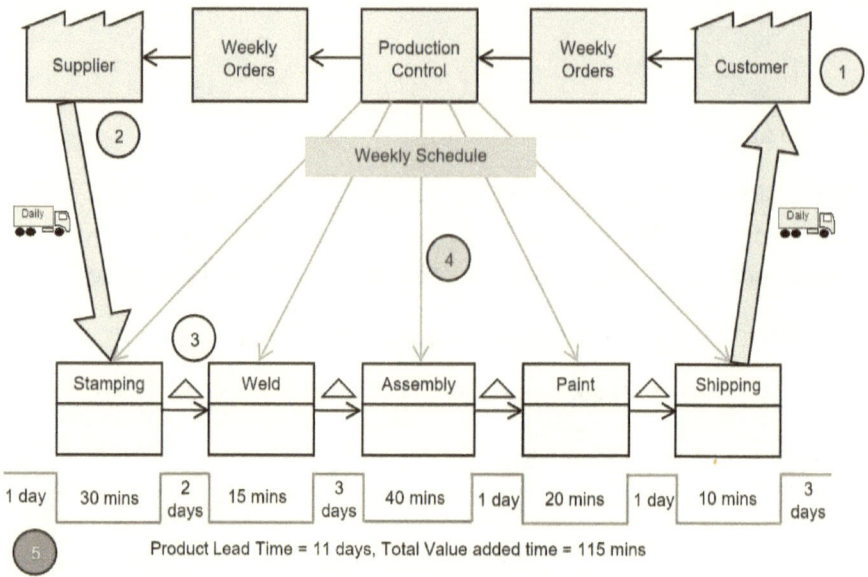

Figure 11.2: Current State VSM

Identify opportunities for Improvement

Sr. No	Indicator	Opportunity
1	High inventories between processes	Reduction in inventory by removing the bottlenecks
2	High downtimes	Improvement in the uptime by the application of TPM (Total Productive Maintenance)
3	High Changeover Time	Reduction in setup time by the application of SMED (Single minute exchange of dies)
4	Lead time much higher than processing time	Creating flow through line balancing and improving the throughput with the same resources

5	Too complex information flow and controls	Streamlining information flow from the customer through Pull system
6	Too much waiting time between processes	Reduction in waiting time through single piece flow wherever possible
7	Too much scrap/rework in the processes	Application of six sigma projects to reduce variation and hence defects
8	Excessive manpower in any process	Elimination of resources by reducing non-value-added activities

Figure 11.3: Opportunities from Current State VSM

A fully finished current state VSM looks like the one in Fig. 11.2. Reviewing the CVSM, we can identify the following improvement opportunities using the table above in Fig 11.3 as the guidelines:

Flow Makers & Flow Detractors

Before we start creating Future state VSM, we shall learn some concepts of Lean manufacturing systems in this section.

Types of Flow:

Flow is mainly of three types:

Information Flow:

1. Everybody knowing hourly production targets

2. How quickly the problems get noticed

3. What happens when there are problems or abnormalities

Product Flow:

The work piece flow from one value adding processing step to next value adding processing step.

Personnel Flow:

1. The operator works with repeatable and consistent manner within each cycle.

2. Can the operator efficiently move from performing one value adding work element to another

Push & Pull System

Push System:

We have briefly introduced the push and pull system in the Lean introduction chapters. However, they are detailed here. In the traditional manufacturing system using process layouts the material is pushed from one process to another by creating large quantity of work in process (WIP) as the schedules are given for each process to produce certain quantity to fully utilize the machines (Ref to Fig 11.4).

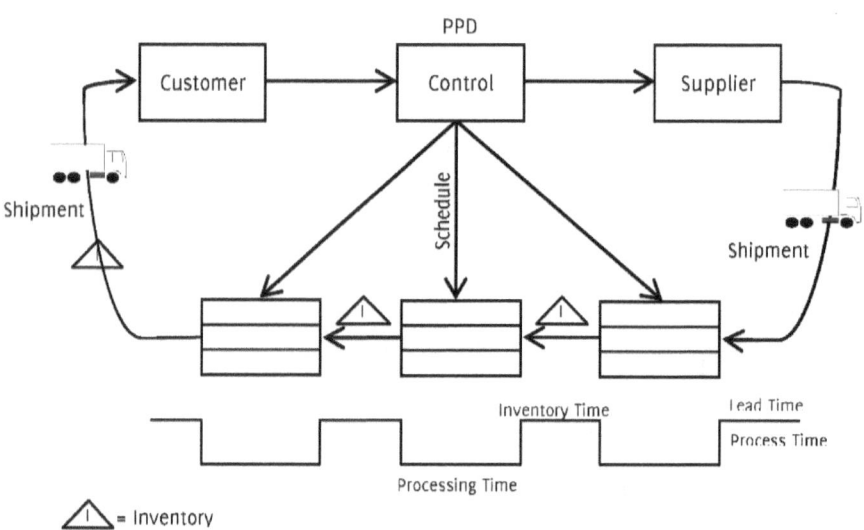

Fig 11.4: Traditional Process Layout – Push System

Pull System:

In the Pull system, the customer order pulls the material along with the processes and delivers it to the customer on time. The cycle time of the processes balanced in such a way there is no inventory buildup between processes. Pull system is also known as single piece flow (SPF) as the operator processes one at a time and passes on to the next process (Ref to Fig 11.5). In a restaurant, we notice the pull system as the system responds only after the customer arrives in the restaurant.

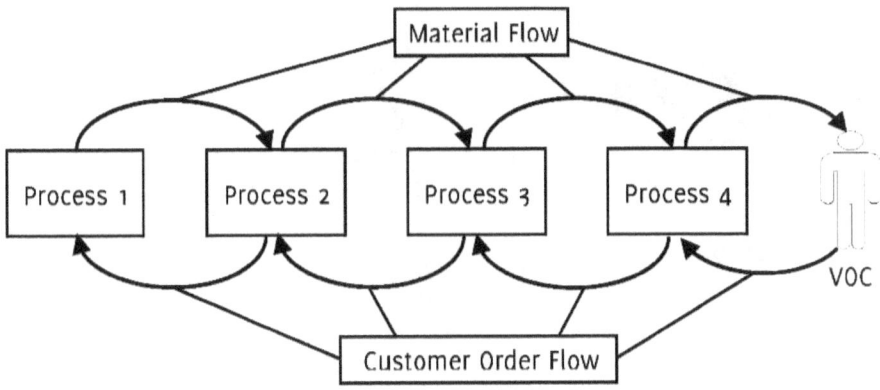

Fig 11.5: Single Piece Flow – Pull System

Flow Detractors:

In creating a Lean manufacturing system eliminating waste, we need to create flow of material without waiting or unnecessarily moving around the shop floor. In the service process, the information/files flow is similar to the material flow in manufacturing. There are few flow detractors which need to be addressed in the Future state value stream using Lean principles. They are briefly explained below:

Batch processing:

The traditional belief is that for the most effective utilization of equipment & people resources, we must have long batches producing similar products of large quantity as the setting time of machines was very high. Often the processes/people were divided into compartments and were given batches of dissimilar parts to make. This is known as batch processing and builds inventory and acts as a flow detractor in the principles of Lean manufacturing system.

Monuments:

Lean aims to produce products only when the customer wants and one at a time. All manufacturing and service processes are not amenable for a single-piece flow due to their inability to produce one at a time such as electroplating, heat treatment in a manufacturing process. A good example of batch processing in a service business is running a computer program for a large data base. These processes which are not very convenient for single-piece flow are called monuments.

Changeover Time:

In a manufacturing system, often the same machine or equipment is used for producing many different parts for different products; for example, the same 30-ton press may be used to produce multiple parts which require different tools to produce them. In the traditional batch processing system, the change over time from one tool to another is not given much importance as it does not matter since the other process always produces parts from the WIP. In the Lean manufacturing system, the flow of material is important, Lean demands quick change over methods often called SMED (Single minute exchange of dies).

Down Time:

Machine down time is the breakdown time of the machines and equipment which are not available for productive purposes. In the traditional push system, the down time may not be of serious consequences but in Pull system as there is no WIP the down time of the equipment will drastically affect the flow of material and hence the customer delivery time. Therefore, Down time is one of the flow detractors that needs to be addressed in a Lean manufacturing system

Un-balanced Line:

The cycle time of any process depends on the way in which the process and tooling is designed. In the push system, where there are many inventories as WIP between processes, it is immaterial that the cycle times are not balanced or there are bottle necks in the processes. But in the Lean manufacturing system where we have single piece flow, it is important to balance the cycle time within the customer demand time which is discussed later in this chapter.

Flow makers:

In this section we shall see some Lean concepts which aid the Flow manufacturing system as single piece flow – SPF which is the primary aim of a Lean manufacturing system.

Cell Layout:

Wherever the product can flow as a single piece across various process steps which have almost equal cycle time can be formed into a cell. A cell has an input and a value-added output and can be managed by one or more operators depending on the technology deployed for the processes.

A typical cell layout is shown below in Fig 11.6:

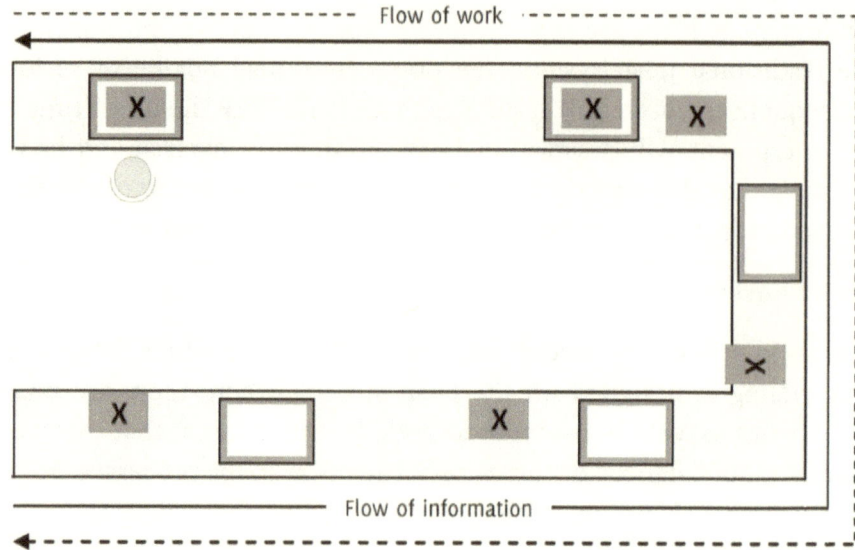

Fig 11.6: Cellular Process Layout

Supermarket:

In an ideal Lean manufacturing system, it is preferred to have all process steps of equal cycle time so that, the material flows are smooth. Often it is not possible as the process cycle times have unequal magnitude and hence, it creates a need for keeping some work in process to keep the flow going without interruptions. A well-planned work in process of predetermined quantity is called 'Supermarket'. (Ref to Fig 11.7)

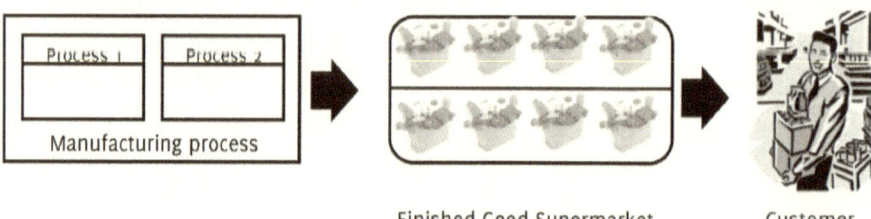

Fig 11.7: Supermarket layout

FIFO – First in First out:

Supermarket is ideal when the products moving from one process to another is of identical type. Just in case, if the product is mixed flow where the subsequent product may be different from the previous one, we need a FIFO method to ensure that the right product is put together in the right sequence. FIFO is applicable when the products are custom build and are not interchangeable. A FIFO system is represented diagrammatically below in Fig 11.8:

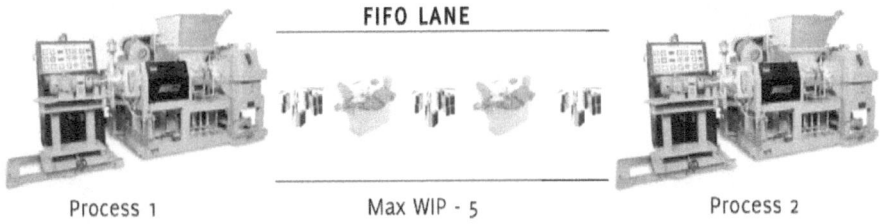

FIFO LANE

Process 1   Max WIP - 5   Process 2

Fig 11.8: FIFO lane

KANBAN:

In the traditional push system using fragmented layouts, products/ parts are manufactured to the schedules given by the production planning department and they are often coordinated using progress chasers on the shop floor (Ref to Fig 11.9). In the Lean manufacturing system, the entire flow from raw material to finished goods happen as a continuous flow without any accumulation of WIP except in supermarkets. In this system, it is important to establish a communication mechanism between the various process steps be it a Cell or supermarket, or monument. This communication system is called 'Kanban' which is a Japanese word for the card as in the early Lean manufacturing system cards are used as communication between the process steps.

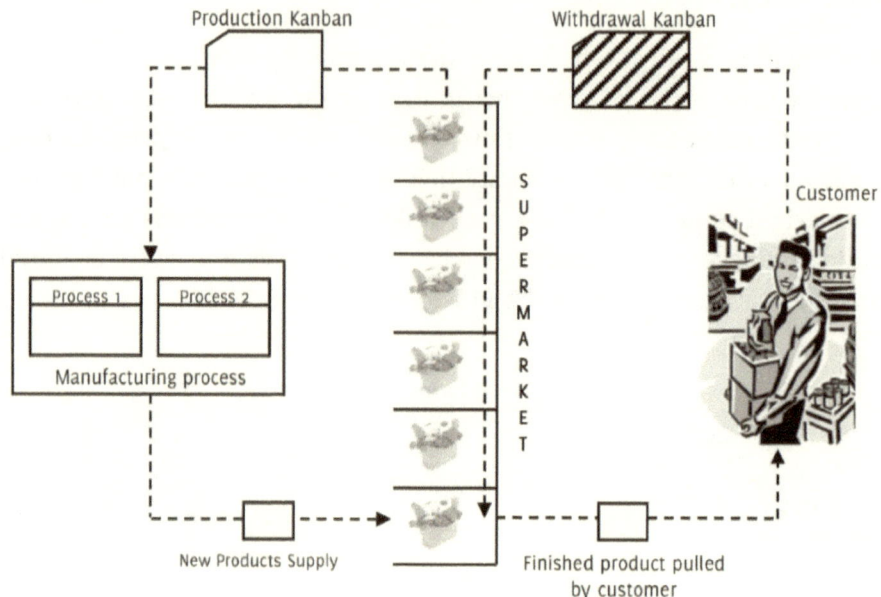

Fig 11.9: Kanban System

There are two types of Kanban namely 'Production Kanban' and 'Withdrawal Kanban'. The production Kanban as the name implies instructs the upstream processes to produce the quantity specified in the Kanban card whereas withdrawal Kanban requests for release of parts from the supermarket as shown in the picture.

Single Piece Flow:

Single-piece flow is the cornerstone of the Lean manufacturing system. It means that all parts and products are produced, by continuously making the material to flow by processing one at a time with zero inventories between processes. A comparison of batch processing and SPF is illustrated below in Fig 11.10:

Batch Processing

Continuous Flow – 'Make One, Move One'

Fig 11.10: Batch Processing vs. Continuous Flow

Lean Manufacturing/Service System Design

In this section, we shall see how we can design a Lean manufacturing/ service system using the Eight step approach for Lean design. Using the eight-step approach we shall develop the Future state VSM which will create a framework for the Lean manufacturing system. The waste elimination happens automatically when we re-design the push system to pull system using these eight steps.

The eight steps are illustrated below in Fig 11.11 and explained in detail subsequently:

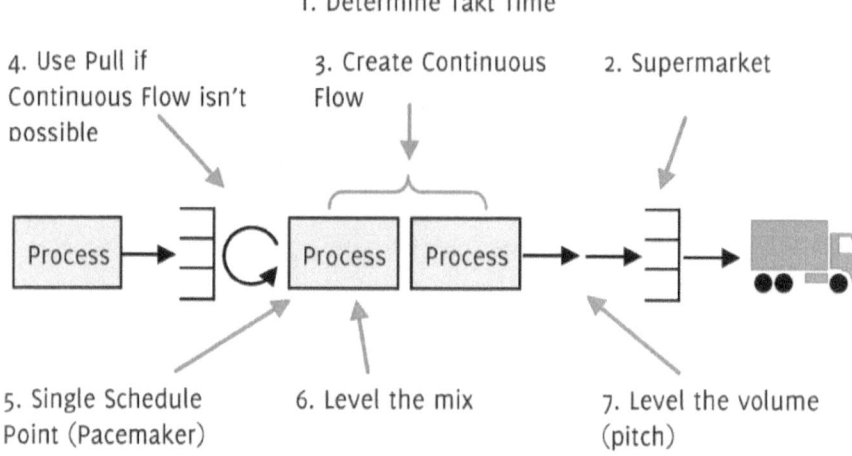

Fig 11.11: 8-Step Approach to Lean System Design

Step-1: Determine the Takt time:

Traditional manufacturing system functions in isolation of processes with their own cycle times and pushes the material into the WIP. The final assembly draws material from the WIP stores and puts them together. In contrast to this, the Lean Pull system has no WIP and must add value through each process continuously keeping the flow till the finished goods are shipped to the customer. Hence, the producing rate has to sync with the asking rate of the customer demand.

In order to achieve this, the Lean system aims to synchronize the processing times with the customer demand rate which is expressed as *'Takt time'* which is the German word for rhythm. The Takt time is like 'Taal' in an orchestra which regulates the other players of the instruments. Similarly, Takt time synchronizes the processes within the manufacturing system.

The Takt time is calculated using the following equation:

Takt time = Available time per day (say 400 minutes) ÷ Customer demand per day (say 100) = 4 minutes

Step-2: Determine FG shipment or Supermarket

The second step is to start from the customer interface point where the shipments have to take place as per the customer needs. Depending upon the fluctuations of the customer demands, we can choose with or without supermarket at the end of the manufacturing line. The choices are illustrated below in Fig 11.12:

Customer Requirements

Customer Despatch with a Supermarket

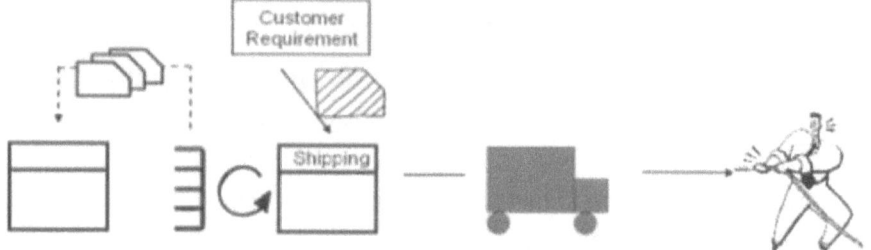

Fig 11.12: Determine shipment

Step-3: Create Continuous Flow

We have been working on the Future state VSM starting from the customer end working through the upstream process steps. The steps followed in creating a flow involves:

1. Aiming to produce one piece at a time as , single piece flow wherever possible.

2. Introduce Supermarket/FIFO wherever Single Piece Flow (SPF) is not possible. This is decided based on the monuments – processes that have to run on batch processing.

3. Form Cells wherever feasible.

4. Balance the line as detailed below.

5. Determine the number of people required in the Lean system.

Line balancing:

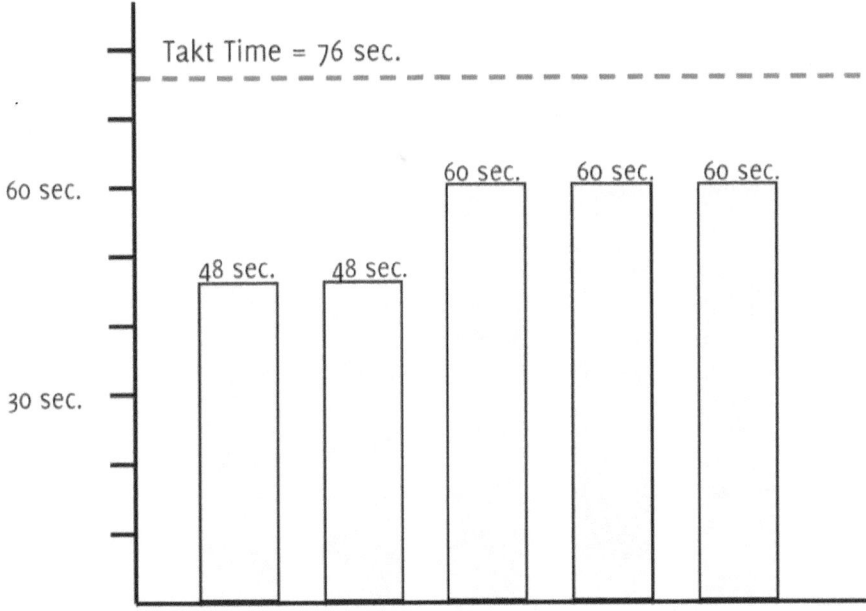

Fig 11.13: Determine Takt Time vs. Cycle Time

The balancing of each process cycle time has to be done against the Takt time as shown above in Fig 11.13. Wherever the cycle time of the process is higher than the Takt time, it will hinder the customer delivery lead time and needs to be further optimized (please refer to Optimize phase for details)

Number of Operators:

The number of people is determined using the following equation:

No of people = Sum of all processing time ÷ Takt time

Note:

If the number of people is greater than 0.5 round it off to the next integer, if it is less than 0.5 round it off to a lesser integer. In such cases, we need to look for optimization opportunities to eliminate few work elements which shall be discussed in the Optimization phase.

Step-4: Use Pull if continuous Flow is not possible

Creating single-piece flow throughout the process from raw material to finished goods may not be possible in many cases as there are processes that have the need to remain as batch processes or we may have unbalanced cycle time. In such cases, we deploy supermarkets to create a flow with minimum inventories. A scenario of such kind is illustrated below in Fig 11.14:

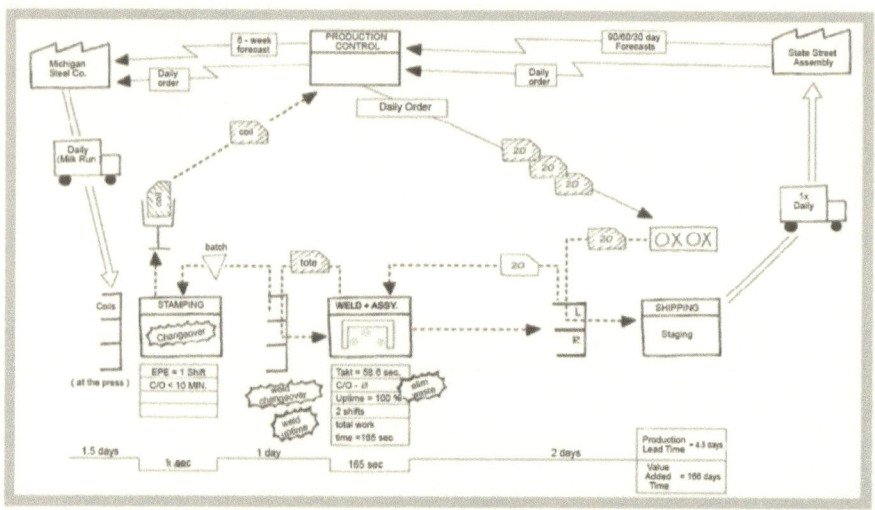

Fig 11.14: Pull system with Supermarket

Step-5: Setting up Pacemaker position:

After setting up the process flow in the FVSM, the next step is to decide which process step the customer order will trigger workflow. This process step is called the 'pacemaker'. As the name implies, this process will set the pull of the rest of the process in a Lean manufacturing system. In a service process like a restaurant, the waiter taking orders acts as a pacemaker. In a manufacturing system, the customer order closer to the dispatch generally chosen as the pacemaker. In FVSM the drum symbol indicates the pacemaker process.

Step-6: Levelling the Production Mix: (Heijunka)

The push system always runs with a single item of large quantity as the set-up times are always very high and hence justified with large batches which end up in inventories. This also makes the customer to wait as the products he wants is always in the queue to be produced. The Lean being a flexible manufacturing system with minimum change over time, it can produce mixed mode of products of smaller quantities. Level scheduling referred as Heijunka in Japanese language aims to plan mixed mode manufacturing as illustrated below in Fig 11.15:

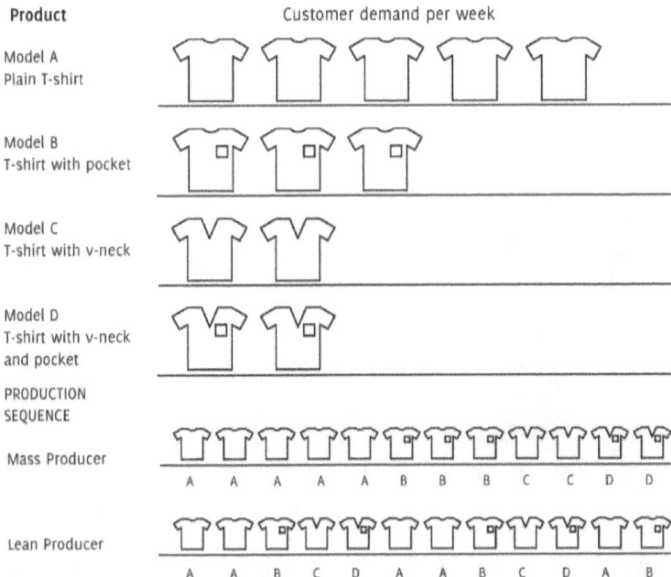

Reference: Lean Lexicon Second Edition October 2004.

Fig 11.15: Heijunka System

In order to trigger production in a mixed mode, Kanban cards are arranged in 'Heijunka box' as shown below in Fig 11.16:

Fig 11.16: Heijunka box

Step-7: Level the Volume (Pitch)

The next step in the Lean FVSM is to decide the number of units that will be triggered by the pacemaker process to suit the customer demand and frequency of dispatch. This is decided by what is known as 'Pitch' in the Lean manufacturing system.

| Parts Factory | Car Factory | Car | Car Dealer |

Pitch is the amount of time needed in a production area to make one container of products. The formula for pitch is:

Pitch = Takt time X pack-out quantity

For example, if the takt time is one minute and the pack-out quantity is 20 pieces, then the pitch is 20 minutes.

Step-8: Improvement to strengthen the Flow:

In spite of creating a framework of the Lean manufacturing system applying Future state VSM, we have not solved all problems to make flow happen absolutely perfect.

This eighth step in Lean design is to list all improvement opportunities that will be addressed in the Optimize phase with the application of Kaizen (small improvements continuously achieved)

The areas of improvements that can be considered are:

1. Reduction in changeover time and batch sizes.

2. Improvement of up time of machines.

3. Eliminate of NVA in the activities of the work cell to reduce the work content time.

4. Teams should be deployed to work on individual projects and a sense of urgency is to be instilled.

5. Determine the number of people required in the Lean system.

CHAPTER 12

Optimize

"How can we optimize the process at the activity levels so that the Pull system has the least amount of waste?"

Why to Optimize the Future State Value Stream?

The future state VSM developed in the Analyze phase has created the Flow of the basic Pull system defining the Cells, supermarkets, FIFOs, Pacemakers, etc. However, the design of the Lean system needs to be detailed to optimize the resources by eliminating waste. The Optimize phase as the name implies ensures that minimum resources are deployed in the Lean manufacturing/service system. Fig 12.1, illustrates Optimize Roadmap.

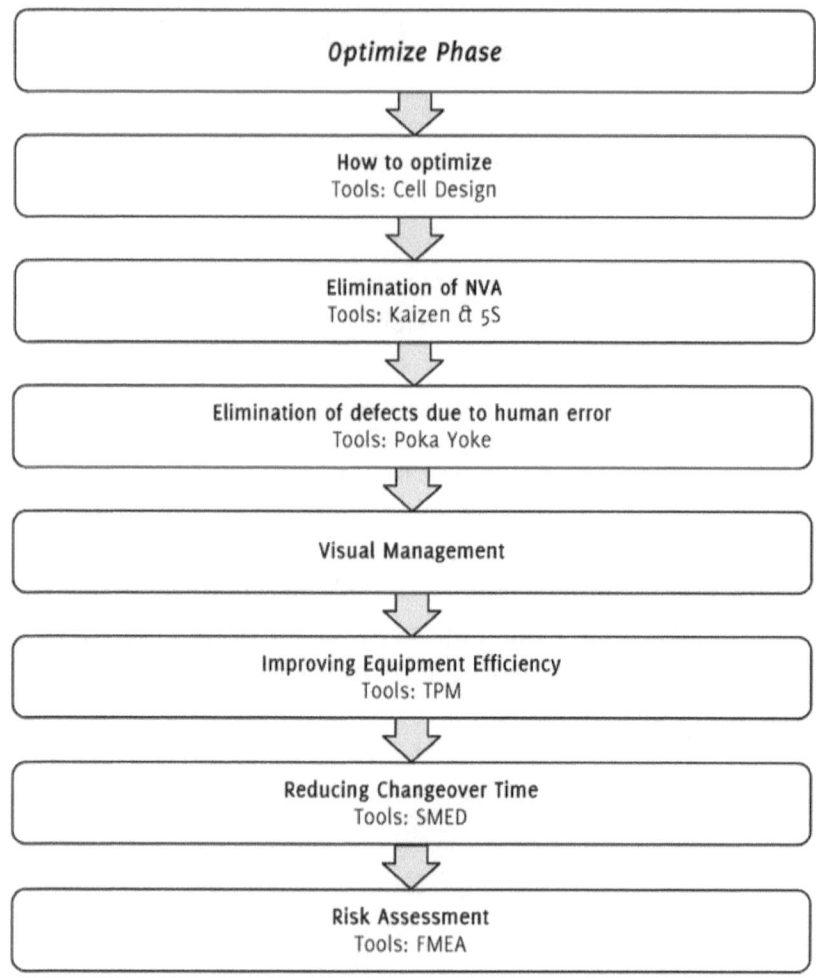

Fig 12.1: Optimize Roadmap

Cell design:

In a Lean manufacturing system, a cell is a self-contained unit with people and processes where a Single-Piece Flow system can be introduced. There can be multiple cells in a manufacturing system which has their own inputs and outputs in sync with the overall material flow from raw material to finished goods. A typical cell is shown in the Fig 12.2.

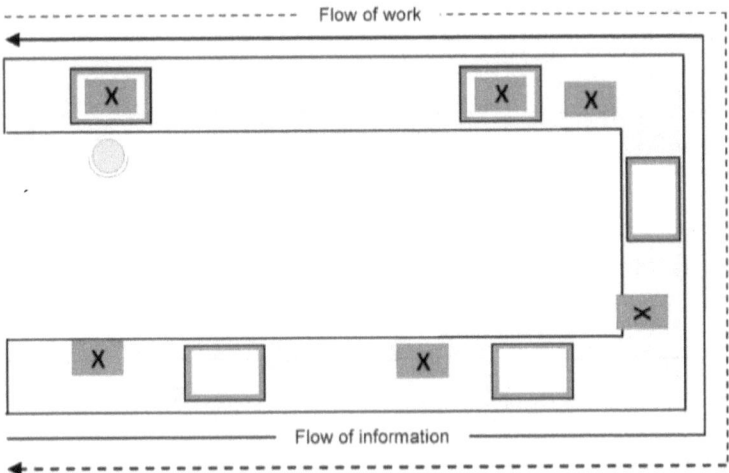

Fig 12.2: Cellular Process Layout

In a functional manufacturing system (Process layout), the product moves from one section to another after waiting for long time in the WIP. Often, the quality problems get highlighted after a huge quantity has been produced. A typical functional manufacturing layout in Fig 12.3 is shown below along with the material movements.

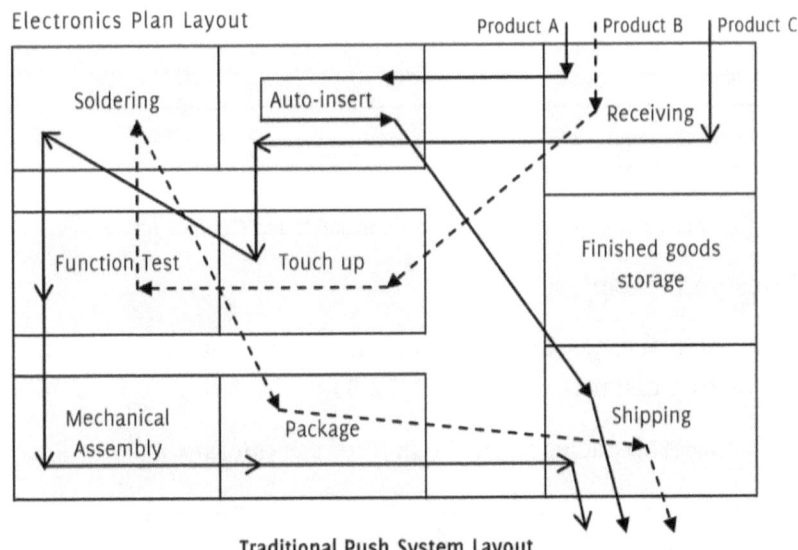

Fig 12.3: Traditional Push System Layout

The comparative benefits of the functional and Cell in a Lean system is listed in a table in Fig 12.4 below:

Key Element	Functional	Cellular
Inter-department moves	Many	Few
Travel distance	500'-4000'	100'-400'
Route structure	Variable	Fixed
Queues	12-30	3-5
Throughput time	Weeks	Hours
Response time	Weeks	Hours
Inventory turns	3-10	15-60
Supervision	Difficult	Easy
Teamwork	Inhibits	Enhances
Quality feedback	Days	Minutes
Skill range	Narrow	Broad
Scheduling	Complex	Simple
Equipment utilization	85% - 90%	70% - 80%

Fig 12.4: Difference between Functional and Cellular layout

Cell Design Principles:

1. Place machines and workstations close together to minimize walking distance. (Ref to Fig 12.5)

2. Remove obstacles from the path of the operators.

3. Eliminate spaces where WIP can get accumulated.

4. Maintain consistent height of work surfaces and points of use.

5. Arrange the Cell in a U-shape to minimize the walking distance from start to the end of the process steps. (Ref to Fig 12.6)

6. Use gravity to assist operators in placing parts and moving materials.

7. Use flexible utility drops from the ceiling to make layout adjustments easier.

8. Use dedicated hand tools instead of tools that require a tool bit changes and combine two or more tools wherever possible.

9. Ensure ergonomics and safety.

10. Keep work instructions and reference manual visible and accessible.

11. Employ multi-skill work force to support all processes in the Cell.

Fig 12.5: Typical self-contained workstations

Fig 12.6: Typical Cell with a U-layout

Eliminate NVA by kaizen and 5S:

In the Analyze phase, we have created a framework of Lean Pull system and in Optimize phase we get into the granularity of the process activities to identify NVAs and eliminate them.

Kaizen:

Kaizen is the continuous improvement tool with small innovations in the process which eliminates the NVAs.

Kaizen is a Japanese word for continuous improvement.

What are the elements of Kaizen?

Quality Circles: Quality circles are the voluntary team of operators, who identify an improvement area in the process and systematically solve those problems.

Teamwork: Kaizen encourages teamwork in problem solving creating a culture of continuous improvement.

Suggestion schemes: It encourages all employees to identify and suggest solutions for the problems that lead to the sense of pride for them.

Kaizen aims at reduction in Lead time from order to delivery by continuously eliminating the NVAs. Fig 12.7 shows the various forms of NVAs.

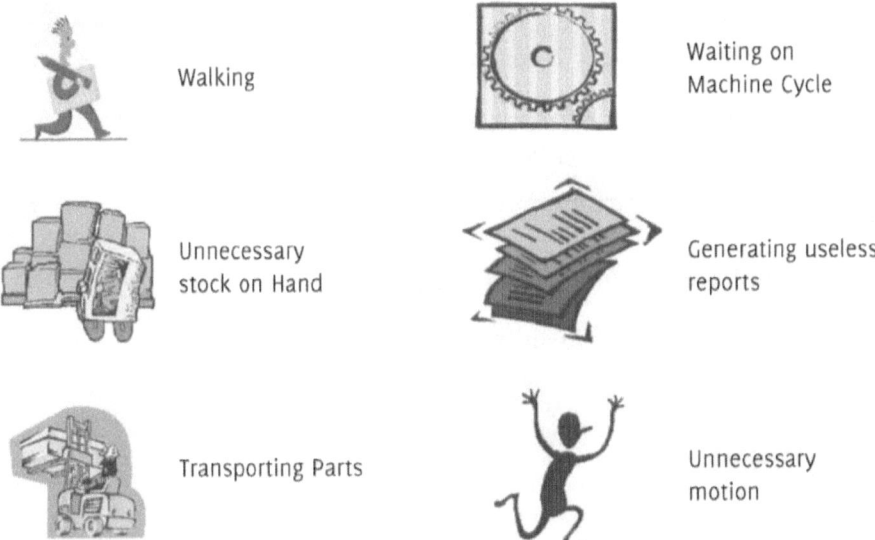

Fig 12.7: Various forms of NVA

How Kaizen solves the problem?

Kaizen uses the systematic problem-solving steps of TQM as given below:

Step-1 Brain Storming

Step-2 Theme and Goal Set-up

Step-3 Data Collection

Step-4 Classification

Step-5 Cause and Effect Analysis

Step-6 Countermeasure Set-up (Plan)

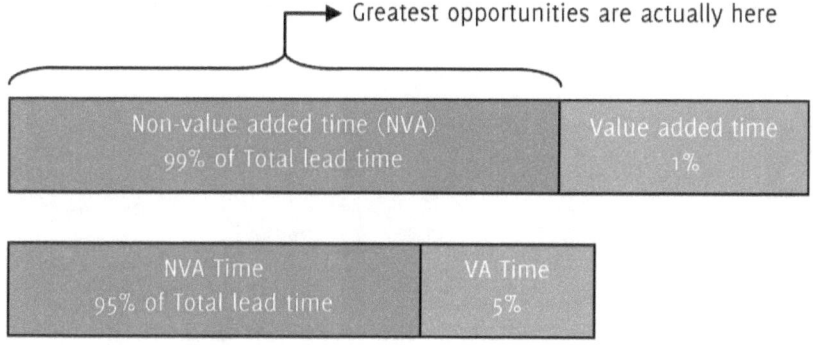

Step-7 Implementation (Do)

Step-8 Effectiveness of Results (Check)

Step-9 Correction of Countermeasure (Action)

Step-10 Monitoring

Step-11 Standardization

5 S:

One of the ways the NVAs can be eliminated is by the application of good housekeeping principles. 5S is the simple 5 step approach suggested by the Japanese quality management system. The 5S stands for:

Seiri – Sort

Seiton – Set in order

Seiso – Shine

Seiketsu – Standardize

Shitsuke – Sustain

These steps are explained in brief below:

Seiri – Sort:

This is the first step in the 5S program where we eliminate all unwanted items from the place of work. This not only refers to the tangible materials but also includes the activities which are waste. A typical list of items that can be thrown away are listed below:

- Faulty tools & equipment
- Unwanted items/tools
- Misallocation
- Unwanted steps/activities
- Motion (just moving around)
- Waiting (Activity)
- Non-moving Inventory/stock
- Defective products
- Transport (Material/information movement)

What is the process to identify the items to be discarded?

The recommended practice is to identify the unwanted item with a red tag as shown below in Fig 12.8 and 12.9:

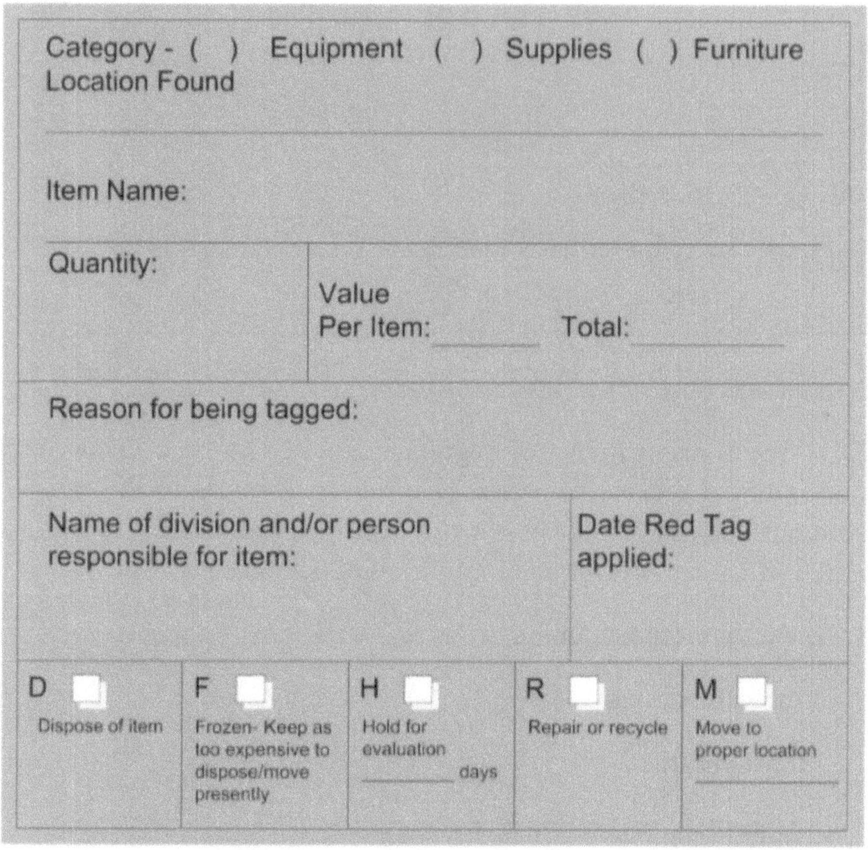

Category - ( ) Equipment ( ) Supplies ( ) Furniture Location Found				
Item Name:				
Quantity:	Value Per Item:_____ Total:_____			
Reason for being tagged:				
Name of division and/or person responsible for item:			Date Red Tag applied:	
D ▢ Dispose of item	F ▢ Frozen- Keep as too expensive to dispose/move presently	H ▢ Hold for evaluation _____ days	R ▢ Repair or recycle	M ▢ Move to proper location

Fig 12.8: Red tag

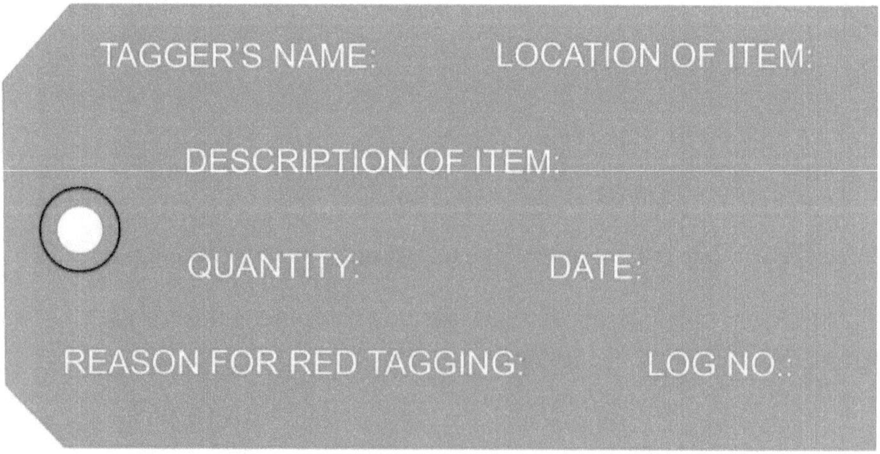

TAGGER'S NAME: LOCATION OF ITEM:

DESCRIPTION OF ITEM:

QUANTITY: DATE:

REASON FOR RED TAGGING: LOG NO.:

The process of elimination is described in the flow chart below in Fig 12.9

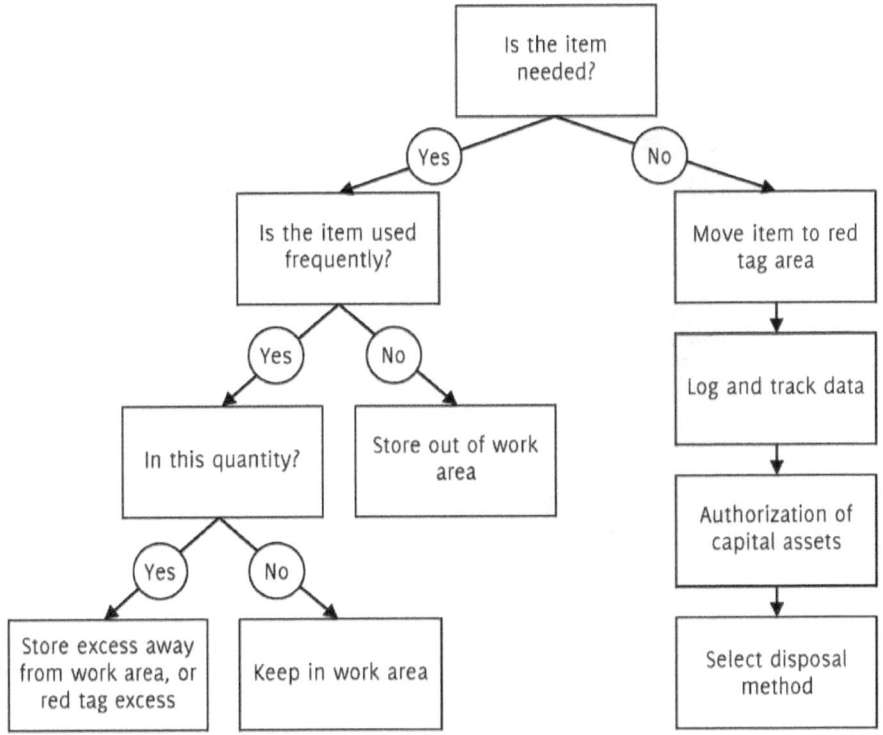

Fig 12.9: Sorting Process

Seiton – Set in Order:

Everything that is movable should have a designated place to be when not in use.

(Ref to Fig 12.10)

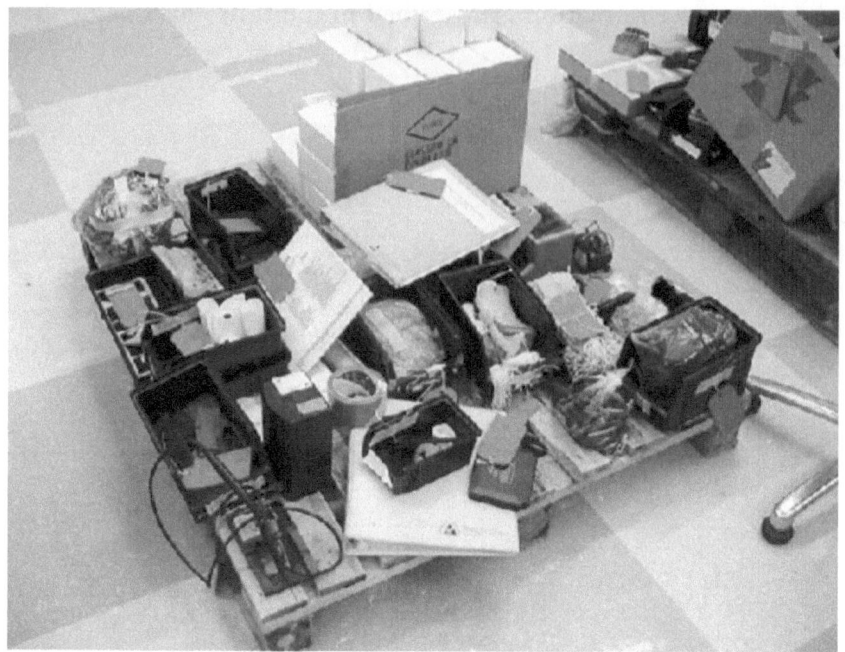

Fig 12.10: Example – A collection of sorted items

Action: arrange items so they are:

- Easy to find

- Easy to use

- Easy to put away (Ref to Fig 12.11)

Tools:

- FVSM (Future State Value Stream Mapping)

- SMED (Single Minute Exchange of Dies)

- Visual Controls

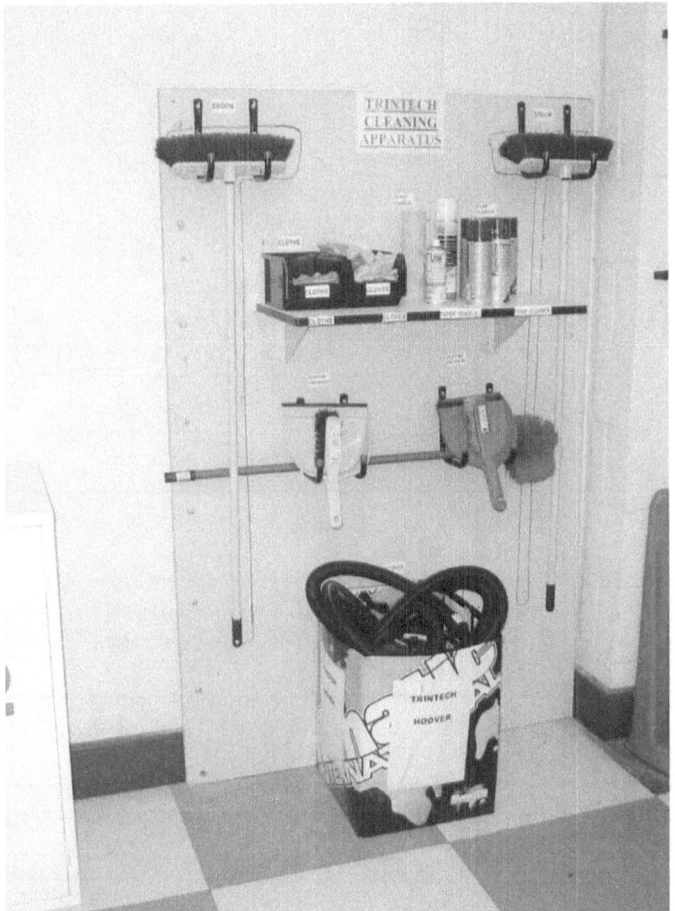

Fig 12.11: Example of 'Place For Everything and Everything in its Place (PEEP)'

Seisu – Shine:

Clean and ready to use

Action:

- Preventive inspection.

- Shine for maintenance.

- Check for quality and safety problems.

- Everything ready to use.

Tools

- Schedule plan

- Working instructions

- Cleaning for needed maintenance

- Red Tag

Planning for Shine: (Illustrated in Fig 12.12)

Targets	Identify tools and equipments in the workplace that need to be included in the Shine process; determine cleaning and inspection frequency for each item
Schedule	Develop a schedule and assign responsibilities; allocate regular time for Shine activities
Methods	Develop standard methods for what will be done, how it will be done, and when. Incorporate inspection methods in standard working procedures
Tools/ Supplies	Identify required tools and supplies and ensure that they are available
Implement	Carry out methods as per the standards and schedules; audit effectiveness

Fig 12.12: Plan for Shine

Seiketsu – Standardize:

Process consistency

- Stabilizes the process

- Minimizes effects of human variability ,

Process Improvement

- Provides a baseline, a foundation for improvement

- Encourages scientific method over Improvement

Training

- Eliminates variation in training
- Makes faster training possible

Guidelines

- Make standards obvious & easy to see from a distance
- Necessary information should be near the operation
- Make standards understandable by anyone
- Use KIS (Keep it simple) approach
- Ensure that standards accomplish their purpose
- Continues Flow
- Visual working environment
- Point of use, availability, proximity.
- Ease of access & return
- Easy to use & to store.
- Frequency of use, visibility
- Standard working instructions
- Two bin system
- Efficient, visual and functional Cell. , (Ref to Fig 12.13)

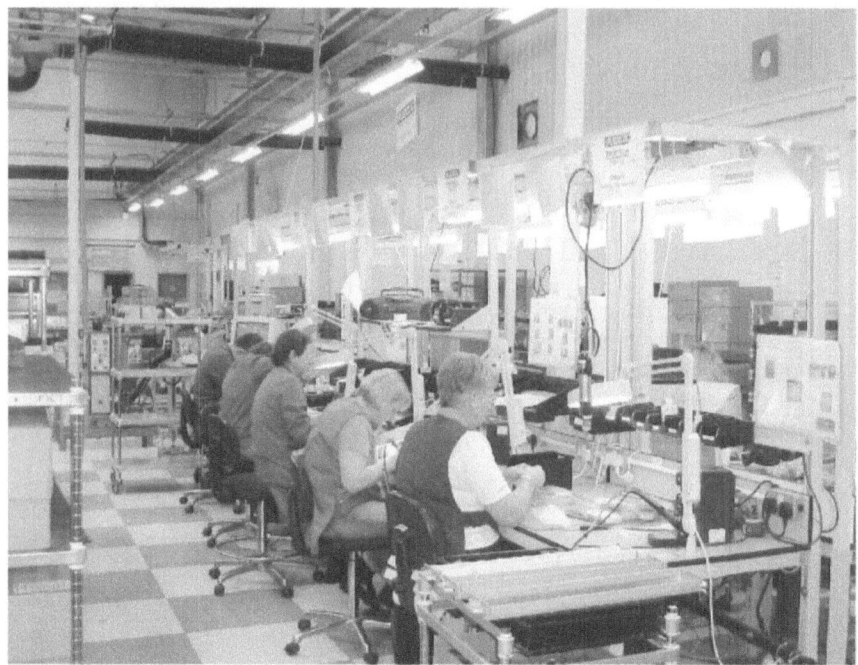

Fig 12.13: Example of a Standardized Cell

Shitsuke – Sustain:

Under lying Concept: Self-discipline and motivation (Ref to Fig 12.14)

Action:

- Awareness and focus
- Recognition
- Satisfaction and enthusiasm

Tools

- Integrated in work instructions
- Dash boards
- Daily routine

- Radar Charts

- Self-audits

- Management Team Quarterly Audits

Keys to Success

- Employee empowerment & buy-in

- Enable Managers to set direction

- Ensure Managers involvement

- Establish routine

- Keep it simple

- Get everyone Involved

Fig 12.14: Example of a 5S System

Elimination of human error (poka-yoke)

The next step in the Optimization phase is to look for opportunity to eliminate human error with the application of mistake proofing techniques called POKE-YOKE in Japanese language. We shall cover this technique more in detail in this section.

What is Poke-Yoke and who invented it?

Fig 12.15: Shigeo Shingo

POKA=ERRORS

YOKE=AVOID

- Poka-yoke is a Japanese improvement strategy for mistake-proofing to prevent defects (or nonconformities) from arising during production processes.

- The Poke-yoke concept was created in the mid-1980s by Shigeo Shingo, a Japanese manufacturing engineer (Ref to Fig 12.15).

- Shingo lists characteristics of poka-yoke devices:

  1. 100 percent inspection is possible.

  2. Devices avoid sampling for monitoring and control

  3. Poka-yoke devices are inexpensive

Why Mistake proofing in Lean?

"Making it easy to do right and impossible to do wrong"

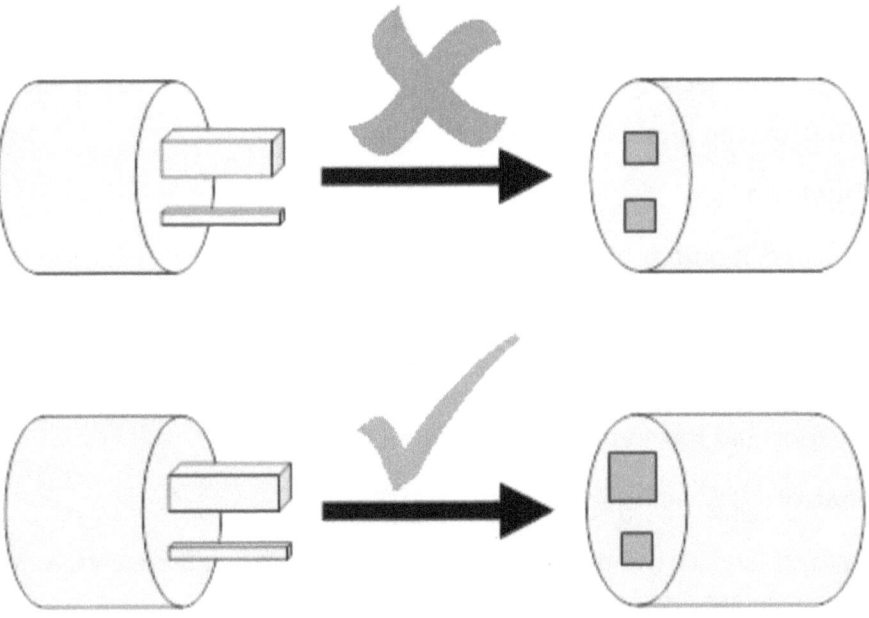

Fig 12.16: Poka Yoke Example

Mistake-proofing: the use of low-cost devices or techniques to perform 100% inspection as a means of eliminating defects. (Ref to Fig 12.16)

1. Assumes that even the most conscientious, well-trained employees will occasionally make errors.

2. Prevents errors from becoming defective products.

3. Is one part of a larger inspection system.

What are the guiding principles in Poke-Yoke?

1. Control upstream, as close to the source of the defects as possible.

2. Establish controls appropriate to severity of potential defect.

3. Don't over control-strive for the most effective and economical control method.

4. Develop cooperatively with operators, technicians and engineers.

5. Don't delay improvement by over analyzing.

What are the methods of mistake proofing?

Shutdown

Effective in both production and detection.

Example: A camera that will not function when there is not enough light to take picture. The meter predicts the light to take a picture and shuts down. Some iron boxes shut down when they detect an overheating situation and thus prevent clothes from damage.

Control

A control device can make pending errors impossible. Erroneous items cannot be used in the process.

Example – A farm assures that only the biggest apple passed on to customers by passing the apples through a sizer. Apples that are too small fall through and are sent to a discount outlet.

Warning

A warning device predicts when something is about to go wrong. It can also sound immediately when something does go wrong.

Example – Seat belt buzzers are warning devices used for prediction. Smoke detectors detect a hazardous situation.

Some Examples of Mistake proofing: (Ref to Fig 12.17, 12.18 and 12.19)

Fig 12.17: Poka Yoke Example

Steps have been labeled as such, presumably to prevent some visitors to hurt themselves or others if they didn't notice the slope and run, cycle or wheelchair down the slope.

Fig 12.18: Poka Yoke Example

The seat belt warning on car dashboards is an arrangement providing a visual alert that a belt is not buckled while the engine is running, or the car is moving

Fig 12.19: Poka Yoke Example

The light is constantly illuminated when switched on, but when in standby the light flashes continuously. It reminds of switching it off after use.

Standardized Work

The next step in the Optimization phase is to develop standardized work. In this section, we shall see what standardized work and why it is needed in Lean manufacturing system.

What is Standardized work?

Lean system believes in self-management by operators with least amount of supervision and inspection. For this purpose, Lean develops a *'Daily work management'* (DWM) system which is possible only when the operator knows the following:

1. What to produce and how to produce?

2. What is the quality requirements and whether they are met or not?

3. When the requirements are not met, how to set right the process and what to do with the non-conforming product produced?

When the above three conditions are met, the operator is self-sufficient and DWM is possible. The standardized work is a visual form which constantly acts as a reminder to the operator to perform the work in a standardized manner.

Elements of Standardized work:

Standard work sequence – This is the order in which a worker must perform tasks, including motions and processes. This is clearly specified to ensure that all workers perform the tasks in the most similar ways possible so as to minimize variation and therefore defects.

Standard timing – Takt time is the frequency with which a single piece is produced. Takt time is used to clearly specify and monitor the rates at which a process should be occurring at various production stages.

Standard in-process inventory – This is the minimum unit of materials, consisting primarily of units undergoing processing, which are required to keep a cell or process moving at desired rate.

What are the contents of Standardized work?

The following contents are recommended:

1. Task details

2. Quality checks

3. Setups

4. Tool changes

5. Routine maintenance performed by operators

6. Any other routine duties , (Ref to Fig 12.21)

Job

1. Each job consists of several tasks.

2. Each made of individual work elements.

Task Details (Content)

1. Explain technical requirements for specific tasks.

2. These are not usually affected by changes in takt time.

3. However, these are the focus of improvement activities.

Work sequence

1. Specifies which tasks should be done by whom and in what order.

2. When takt time changes, the sequence most likely will also change.

A typical format is given below in Fig 12.20:

Standardized Work Combination Table	From: Get SS Tube			Date: June 4, 2008			Needed units per shift		690	Hand Walk Auto							
	To: Finish line to container			Area: Truck Cell			Takt Time		40 sec.								
Work Elements	Time (sec.)			Seconds													
	Hand	Auto	Walk	5 10 15 20 25 30 35 40 45 50 55 60 65 70 75 80 85													
1 Get SS Tube, place to bender	3		1														
2 Get bent tube, place to assembly	3																
3 Get connector, place and clamp	4																
4 Get hose, place	4																
5 Start Assembly I cycle	1		1														
6 Get finished piece, attach convolute	6																
7 Place to Assembly II fixture	5																
8 Get hose, LH ferrule, assemble	4																
9 Place to fixture, clamp	3																
10 Get RH ferrule, assemble to hose	3																
11 Place and clamp	3																
12 Get valve, place to fixture	3																
13 Start Assembly II cycle	1		1														
14 Get finished piece, place to fixture	5																
Totals				5 10 15 20 25 30 35 40 45 50 55 60 65 70 75 80 85													

Ref: Lean Lexicon Second Edition October 2004.

Fig 12.20: Standard Work Table

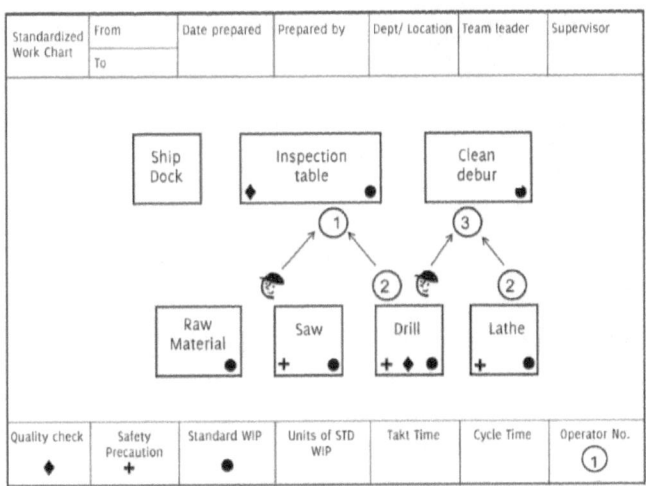

Ref: Lean Lexicon, Second Edition, October 2004

Fig 12.21: Standard Work Flow

Visual management (Andon)

What is visual management & why it is needed?

A visual management tool highlights the status of the operations in an area at a glance and that signals whenever an abnormality occurs. Andon is a Japanese word for 'Lamp'. An Andon can indicate production status (which machine is operating), an abnormality (which machine has stopped or has a quality problem) and needed action as changeover. Andon can also indicate how many units have been produced as against the planned. Examples of ANDON are given below in Fig 12.22:

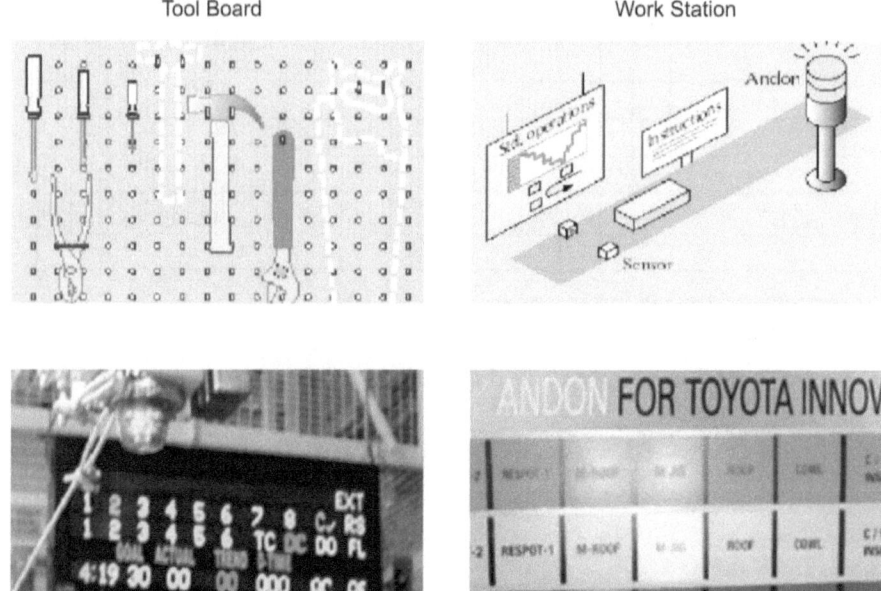

Fig 12.22: Examples of ANDON

Improving equipment efficiency – TPM (Total Productive Maintenance)

The optimization of equipment efficiency to get maximum uptime is very important to get an un-interrupted flow in a Lean manufacturing system. Unlike process layout where there will be enough inventory to keep the downstream processes running, Lean runs on almost zero inventory and hence the need for 100% uptime of the machines and equipment.

What is Total Productive Maintenance (TPM)?

TPM is a set of techniques originally pioneered by Denso in Toyota group in Japan, to ensure that every machine in a production process always able to perform its required tasks. The approach is termed total in three senses; first it requires total participation of all employees, second it seeks the total productivity of the equipment and third it addresses the total life cycle of the machines.

Total Productive Maintenance (TPM) addresses all the six major losses that plague the machine namely down time, changeover time, minor stops, speed losses, scrap, and rework.

Total Productive Maintenance (TPM) Goals are illustrated in Fig 12.23:

Loss	Goal	Description
Breakdowns	0	Zero for all equipment
Setups	Minimize	‹10 min., no adjustments
Minor stoppages	0	Zero for all equipment
Reduced speed	0	Speed should equal or be better than machine specifications
Defects	0	Zero for all equipments
Startup loss	Minimize	Set standards

Fig 12.23: TPM Goals

Five Pillars of Total Productive Maintenance (TPM) are illustrated in Fig 12.24:

Pillars	Description
Eliminate the six big losses	Improve equipment effectiveness
Autonomous maintenance	Operator involvement in maintaining and improving equipment effectiveness
A planned maintenance system	Improve the use of preventive maintenance practices
Improve equipment and maintenance skills	Improve the skills of operators and maintenance personnel
Product maintenance design and early equipment management	Design equipment that requires less maintenance and manage the startup of new equipment

Fig 12.24: Pillars of TPM

What is Total Productive Maintenance (TPM) Targets?

1. Obtain minimum 80% OPE (overall plant effectiveness)

2. Obtain minimum 90% OEE (Overall equipment Effectiveness)

3. Run the machines even during lunch (Lunch is for operator and not for machines!)

4. Operate in a manner, so that there are no customer complaints

5. Reduce the manufacturing cost by 30%

6. Achieve 100% success in delivering the goods as required by the customer

7. Maintain an accident-free environment

8. Increase the suggestions by 3 times.

9. Develop multi-skilled and flexible workers

How the effectiveness of Total Productive Maintenance (TPM) is measured?

The effectiveness of Total Productive Maintenance (TPM) measure is calculated using OEE (Overall Equipment Effectiveness). OEE is calculated from three elements:

1. **The availability rate** measures down time losses from the machine failures & adjustments as a percentage of scheduled time.

2. **The performance rate** measures the operating speed losses – running lower than design speed.

3. **The quality rate** expresses losses due to scrap & rework as a percentage of total output.

Thus, Overall Equipment Effectiveness (OEE) is calculated as:

OEE = Availability rate X Performance rate X Quality rate

If for example availability is 90%, Performance is 95% and quality rate is 99%, then:

OEE = 0.90 x 0.95 x 0.99 = 84.6%

Benefits of Total Productive Maintenance (TPM):

1. Increased productivity and OPE (Overall Plant Efficiency)

2. Customer complaints reduction.

3. Reduced manufacturing cost.

4. Customer's needs satisfied. (Delivering the right quantity at the right, time, in the required quality)

5. Reduced accidents.

Reducing change over time – Single Minute Exchange of Die (SMED)

The next step in Optimization is to explore the possibility of reducing changeover time. In the process layout with Push system, the tooling is designed to consume long time to install and set them in the machine and often they are run for long period of time to justify the loading & set-up time. This approach builds large quantity of WIP as machine utilization was the measure for the efficiency and often justified.

What is Single Minute Exchange of Die (SMED)?

SMED is an acronym for 'Single minute exchange of die'. The key insight about setup time reduction is by separating internal setup operations from external set up operations. The internal set up operation refers to the activities that can be done only when machine is stopped (such as inserting a new die). The external set up operation is any activity that can be performed while the machine is running. SMED technic aims to convert 'Internal operations' to 'External operations'. One such example could be transporting the die to the machine or pre-heating. This is illustrated in the following diagram:

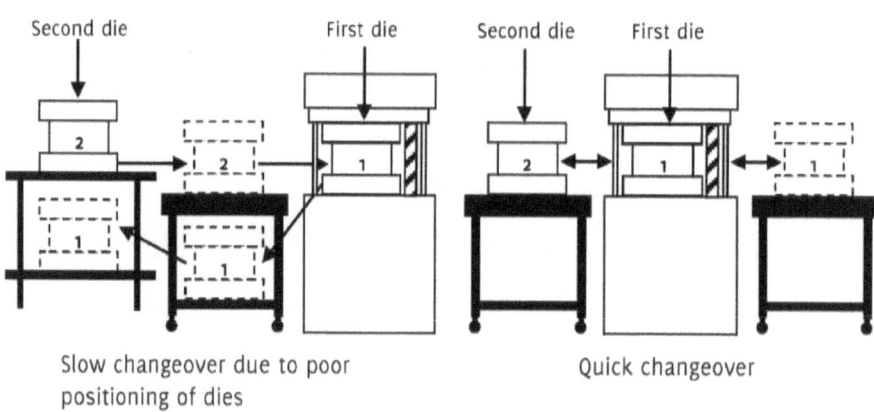

Slow changeover due to poor positioning of dies

Quick changeover

Reference: Lean Lexicon Second Edition October 2004

Fig 12.25: Example – Reduction in changeover time

Why Single Minute Exchange of Die (SMED)?

1. Change from Traditional manufacturing practices to Lean manufacturing practices.

2. Lesser & lesser batch sizes required to run.

3. Reduction in Lead times.

4. Reduce non-value-adding activities.

5. Reduce fatigue involved in long setups.

6. Improve safety.

7. Improve employee morale.

8. Setup time reduction helps – reduce setup cost, allow small lot production, smoothen flow and Improve pull system.

Risk assessment – FMEA

The final step in the Optimize phase is to assess the risk involved in implementing the Lean manufacturing system which is carried out using FMEA – Failure Mode & Effect Analysis.

Failure Mode Effect Analysis (FMEA)

It is an advanced quality planning tool, used to evaluate potential failure mode and their causes. FMEA presents an opportunity to identify the problem but does not solve them. The use of FMEA in analyze phase, helps in identifying the weak points or links in the as-Is process.

Terminologies in FMEA

Failure: It means a component or system not meeting or not functioning to its design intent.

Example:- Malfunctioning in dispensing the notes in an ATM of a bank.

Failure Mode: A failure mode is the way a component or system failure occurs.

Example:- Notes not being dispensed/wrong denomination/wrong amount dispensed.

Effect: The consequences of the failure

Example:- Customer unable to withdraw the required amount/ Customer withdraws incorrect amount.

Severity: Assessment of the seriousness of the effect of the potential failure mode

In a scale of 1-10 the higher the number indicates higher the severity

Occurrence: Likelihood that a specific cause will occur

In a scale of 1-10 the higher the number indicates the probability of occurrence of the event is higher.

Detection: Ability of the system to detect potential failure mode

In a scale of 1-10 the higher the number indicates the detection of the failure mode is difficult.

Risk Priority Number: This number is used to place priority on items that require additional quality planning

RPN = Severity x Occurrence x Detection

Guidelines for FMEA

1. List the process steps in the first column of a chart.

2. For each process step, brainstorm potential failure modes – ways in which the product, service, or process might fail (e.g., slowups, breakdowns)

3. Identify the potential consequences or effects of each failure (e.g., defective product, wrong information, delays) and rate their severity.

4. Identify causes of the failure and rate their likelihood of occurrence.

5. Rate your ability to detect each causes (in the Detection column)

6. Multiply the three numbers (severity, occurrence, and detection) together to determine the risk of each failure mode. This is represented in the chart by a risk priority number, or RPN.

7. Identify ways to reduce or eliminate risk associated with high RPNs.

8. Re-score those failures after you put counter-measures on place.

NOTE: Refer appendix for FMEA template.

CHAPTER 13

Repeat (Maintainability)

How can we stick the lean system and institutionalize the practices?

Why repeatability phase?

All the efforts taken in implementing Lean manufacturing system, we must sustain its benefits and should become a way of life. As shown in the figure 13.1, the improvements slide down over a period of time if not properly maintained through control systems. Although the Lean system is irreversible in design, people may try to get back to the old way of producing things due to shear habit. Hence, the measurement and monitoring system should ensure that the improvements are sustained.

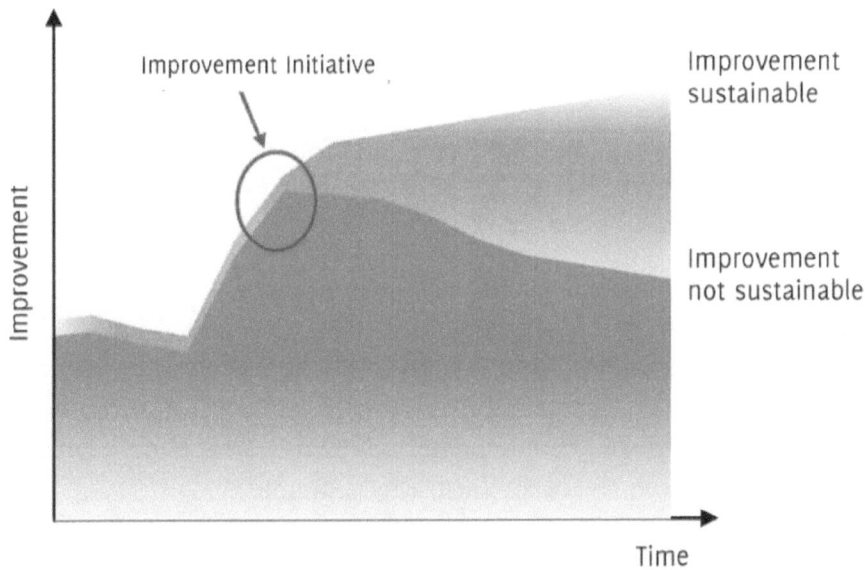

Fig 13.1: Improvement Lifecycle

Repeatability roadmap (Ref to Fig 13.2)

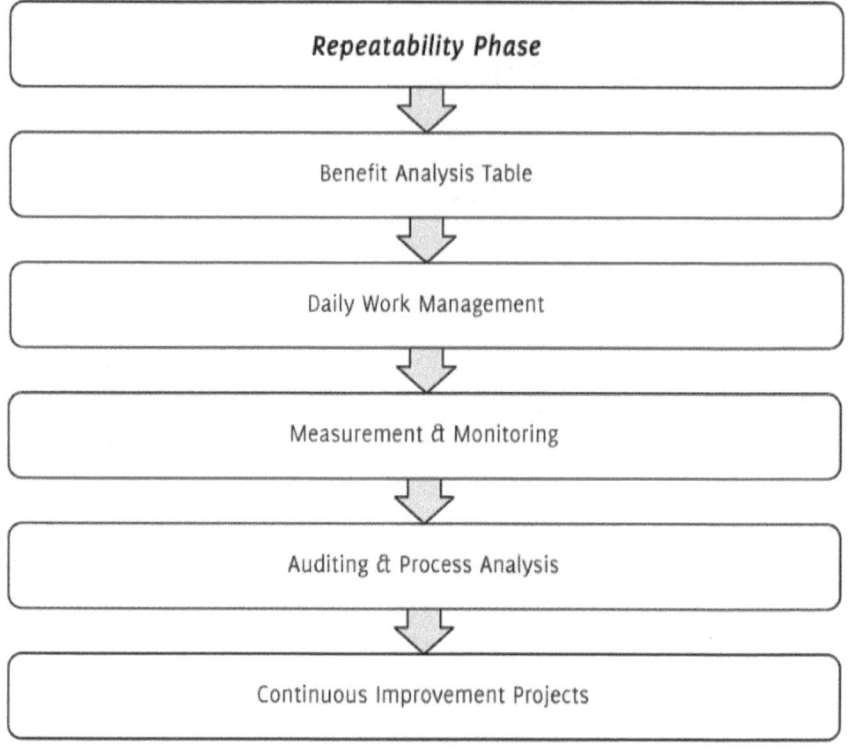

Fig 13.2: Repeatability Roadmap

Benefit Analysis Table: (BAT)

We need to estimate the benefits of Lean manufacturing system over the earlier batch processing system in order to get the buy-in from the people which will help to sustain the benefits of the new system. Lean manufacturing system brings down the cost of manufacture substantially through the parameters shown in the benefit analysis table (BAT). (Table 13.3 is an illustrative example)

Benefit Analysis Table			
Sr. No	*Benefit Attribute*	*Old Process*	*New Process*
1	Improvement in productivity	250 tons/ month	550 tons/ month
2	Reduction in lead time	3 days	5 hours
3	Reduction in inventory	20 tons	5 tons
4	Reduction in floor space	Congested	20% free space
5	Inventory turnover ratio	5	10
6	Turnover per employee	1 Lac	1.5 Lac
7	Process cycle efficiency	2%	4%
8	Total no. of activities	10	7

Fig 13.3: Benefit Analysis Table

Daily Work Management: (DWM)

Lean system believes in self-management by operators with least amount of supervision and inspection. For this purpose, Lean develops a Daily work management (DWM) system which is possible only when the operator knows the following:

1. What to produce and how to produce?

2. What is the quality requirements and whether they are met or not?

3. When the requirements are not met, how to set right the process and what to do with the non-conforming product produced?

When the above three conditions are met, the operator is self-sufficient and DWM is possible. The standardized work is a visual form that constantly acts as a reminder to the operator to perform the work in a standardized manner.

(Please also refer Standardized work in Optimize phase for developing visual aids)

Measuring & Monitoring:

There are two level measurements can be adopted for assessing the effectiveness of the Lean manufacturing system namely:

1. KPI – Key Performance Index

2. Process level MOP (Measure of Performance),

The KPI is a high-level measurement such as:

1. Productivity per employee

2. Production against capacity

The Process level MOPs are such as:

1. Rejects & rework levels

2. DPMO (defects parts per million),

If the process capabilities are established minimum Cp value of 1.33, control charts can be applied for the key process parameters.

Auditing & Process Analysis:

The auditing process can detect adherence to the standardized work and daily work management guidelines and escalate production problems leading to an improvement project. As the Lean manufacturing system has eliminated inspection at each stage through self-inspection and control, we can deploy those resources for daily, weekly and monthly audits as per the standardized checklist.

Response Plans are recommended to guide DWM as well as audit. A response plan is a document that details the manufacturing quality control measures to ensure first time right parts are produced.

A typical response plan is given in the appendix 3.

Continuous Improvement Projects:

However way the Lean manufacturing system is designed, it is not possible to eliminate all wastes in the beginning. During the course of running the Lean system, often we will identify:

1. Problems that restricts the smooth flow of material

2. Quality rejects and rework

3. Non-Value-Added activities

Part of the work culture in the Lean manufacturing system, we need to train people and institutionalize the continual improvement projects to solve the above problems through the people who are responsible for running the production.

For this purpose, Toyota pioneered a practice of identifying the problem, analysis and the corrective action on a single sheet of large A3 paper often with the use of graphics. At Toyota it is called A3 Report which is used for summarizing problem-solving exercises and status reports. A typical A3 report is given in the appendix 2.

Epilogue

It is time to conclude the book on this amazing ideology, methodology & tool about "LEAN" which has revolutionized the way in which business leaders think and run their business. Lean is not an incremental improvement tool, but a major shift in the paradigm of 'Industrial management' practices. In the last 150 years, the world witnessed the pinnacle of technology and inventions that have completely revolutionized the way we live today. The only thing that does not change is change itself and resistance to change is a good recipe to perish. In the last two years, mankind has witnessed the worst calamity of pandemic ever happened in the last 2000 years destabilizing everything on earth. This is a forced change by nature as human beings will surmount all challenges of nature till we are destined to stay before extinct. As the human race is the most evolved and thinking species, we will find more and more efficient ways of setting up a business model that suits the customer's needs.

In the last century alone, many thought leaders have brought many new paradigms that constantly moved the enterprises towards perfection. Some of them are listed below:

1. Six sigma for defect elimination

2. Theory of Constraints (TOC) for removing constraints.

3. DDMRP (Demand Driven MRP) for inventory optimization

4. ISO 9000 for quality assurance

5. Business Excellence models such as EFQM for overall development of the enterprise.

6. TQM to apply quality philosophy across every aspect of the enterprise.

7. Lean manufacturing to improve Return on investment (ROI)

Each one of them is intended to improve the competitiveness of the enterprise and they are not competing but in fact, complementing each other. As I mentioned in the Part-1 of this book, the business leaders need to select and apply these interventions depending upon the maturity of their enterprise. Lean is not a short-term intervention but a major lifesaver in a critical phase the industries are facing today. Everything shall become complex in the future including customer demand for variety and functionality. This demands a very sharp responsiveness of the enterprise which can be achieved only by becoming more agile. Since lean is intended for improving agility, it is often called an "Agile manufacturing system". Agility improves when the unnecessary fat from the system is removed. Hence, Lean is a 'Religion' or way of life that constantly improves the agility of the supply system. It is like doing physical exercise in the gym to create muscle memory to remain agile.

I titled this book as "ENIGMA OF LEAN" due to its mystical nature grossly misunderstood and poorly applied. I am sure you would have demystified this concept a bit now if you would have read the book this far.

You must have enjoyed learning this powerful tool called LEAN which has revolutionized the manufacturing practices of motor car manufacturing, giving tremendous cost-effectiveness. Lean gave the advantage to Toyota, to become the largest car manufacturer in the world reaching the market capitalization exceeding many giants in the west put together. This would not have been possible without the power of Lean which eliminated wastes and meets the customer expectations at the same time.

Although Lean as a concept came from manufacturing discipline, it is extensively applied in service processes worldwide. After all any value creation to the customer, be it manufacturing or service, it involves a set of processes interacting with each other to create value to the customer. The essential difference is the material flows in a manufacturing process and information flows in a service process. In the last 52 years of my exposure in manufacturing companies in automobile & ancillary in different capacities and hands on application of Lean in many industries across the globe as a consultant, I experienced a phenomenal financial benefit to the industries that believed and applied Lean across their entire value stream. Hence, I recommend Lean as an important board room strategy for profitability & sustainability.

Wish you happy reading!

Explore the wealth of Lean to wage a "War on Waste"

Good Luck and Thank you!

– N C Narayanan
Author

Appendix – 1

Lean Charter

Project Name	ABC Lean Implementation	*Business/ Location*	Malaysia Unit
Sponsor	Mr. XYZ	*Project Lead*	Mr. EFG
Start Date	August 2008	*Target End Date*	October 2008
	Product Details		
Project Description	Productivity improvement and inventory reduction		
Business Case	There is a huge demand from the maker for Printed Circuit Boards. The customer will go to a different PCB supplier if they are unable to meet the demand. ABC need to increase the throughput without much capital investment		
Problem Statement	ABC makes 2 lacs of single sided PCB's per month. The demand is 6 lacs PCB per month. 30 days worth WIP is present in the system. Increasing productivity and decreasing WIP will give ABC a huge benefit of shorter lead time and profitability.		
Process Owner	Mr. XYZ		
Scope	Start:	Cut Panels	
	Stop:	Despatch to punching operation	
	Exclude:	Punching and despatch to customer	

Appendix – 2

A3 Report

APEXTUBE COMPANY - Continuous Flow Project

Truck Fuel - Line Pacemaker Cell

1) Background/ Business Case ◄──── *Be sure to link your plan to business objectives*

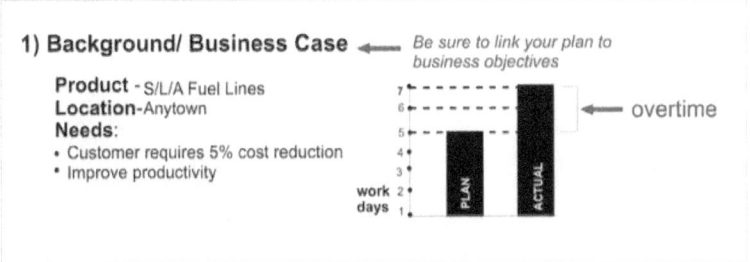

Product - S/L/A Fuel Lines
Location - Anytown
Needs:
- Customer requires 5% cost reduction
- Improve productivity

2) Initial condition

- No continuous material flow
- No people flow (operators stay at one machine)
- Unstable output
- Too much overtime
- Not working to takt time
- Too many operators for demand rate

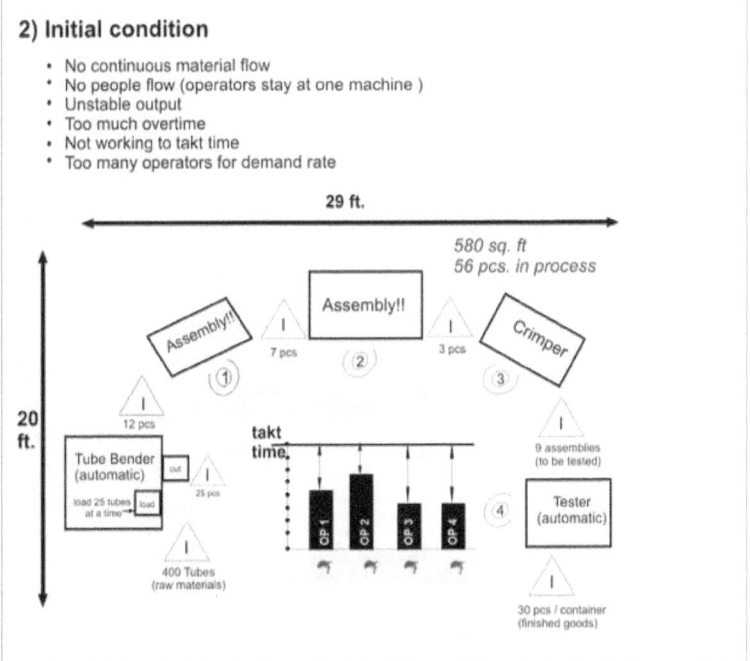

Appendix 2 - A3 Report

3) Target Condition

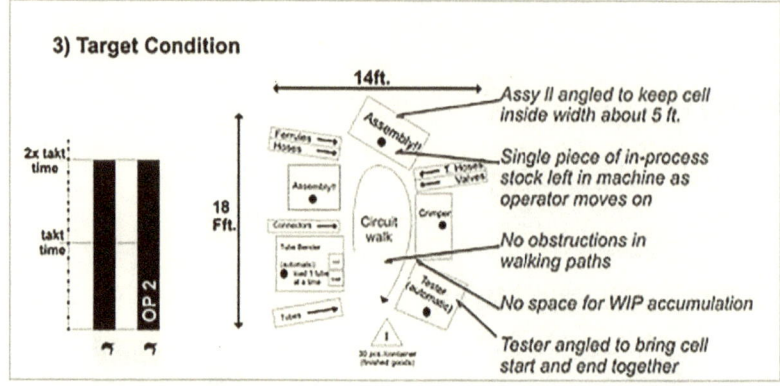

- Assy II angled to keep cell inside width about 5 ft.
- Single piece of in-process stock left in machine as operator moves on
- No obstructions in walking paths
- No space for WIP accumulation
- Tester angled to bring cell start and end together

4) Implementation

#	Task	Metric	Responsible Person	Target date	March 04	April 04	May 04	June 04	Review	Review
1	Introduction Training				○△				○	
2	Mock Up/T rial				○△				○	
3	Add Auto Eject					○—○—△			△	
4	Reconfigure Cell					○—△			○	
5	Std W ork Training					○—△			○	
6	Train Material Handlers					○—△			△	
7	Cell Debugging					○—	?			
8	Finished Goods Supermarket					○—△				
9	Production Kanban					○—△				
10	Frequent Withdrawal						○——△			
11	Heijunka Box							○—		

○ Proposed Start   △ Proposed Completion   ○ On Target   x Trouble

● Actual Start   ▲ Actual Completion   △ Behind Target

(Planning / Tracking)   Review   (Evaluation)

5) Indicators

	Pcs per Hour	WIP	Space	Cost per Unit
Current	20	56 pcs	580 ft	# 8.27
Goal	40	5 pcs	252 ft	# 7.27

Be sure to include goals so level of success can be evaluated.

Ref: Lean Lexicon, Second Edition, October 2004

passion for impossible

Appendix – 3

Response Plan

Response Plan Number			Organization Name/ Site			Key Contact					
Issue Date			Revision Date			Customer Information					

| Process Step Number | Process Name | Checklist/ Dashboard, Reports, etc. | Characteristics | | | Specification / Tolerance | Evaluation Measurement Technique | Method | | | | Reaction Plan | Corrective Action |
			No	Product/ Service	Process			Control Method	Error Proofing	Sample Size	Frequency		

Appendix – 4

Tool Phase Matrix

Tools	Recognize (R)	Map & Measure (M)	Analyze (A)	Optimize (O)	Repeatability (R)
Product Family Matrix	●				
Spaghetti Diagram		●			
Value Stream Map		●			
Process Map		●			
Lean Charter		●			
Heijunka			●		
Cell Design				●	
Kaizen				●	
5S				●	
Poka Yoke				●	
Standard Work				●	
Total Productive Maintenance				●	
Single Minute Exchange of Die (SMED)				●	
Failure Mode Effective Analysis (FMEA)				●	
Benefit Analysis Table					●
Daily Work Management					●

Appendix – 5

Failure Mode & Effect Analysis

Process Step	Potential Failure Mode	Potential Failure Effects	Severity	Potential Causes	Occurrence	Current Controls	Detection	RPN	Actions Recommended
What is the process Step?	What can go wrong with the process step	What is the impact on the customer (the effect on the big Y's)	How severe is the effect to the customer?	What causes the process step to go wrong – what is the source of the failure?	How often does cause or failure mode occur?	What are the existing controls and procedures that either prevent or detect the cause or the failure mode?	How well do you detect cause or failure mode?	Sev X Occ X Det	What are the actions for eliminating or reducing the occurrence of the cause, or improving detection of the cause or failure mode?

Case Studies

Case Study – 1

Project Title: Reduction in TAT for processing of application.

Scenario:

NYK is a facilitation center for processing credit card applications. The process starts after the application has been received from the customer. As per the SLA (service level agreement), any application with TAT greater than 2 days for processing, after the date of receipt of the application, will be considered as a defect.

What was the problem?

The process step for processing the application consists of collecting the application from the customer, verifying the details & documentation and sending the details for printing. Data collected for the previous 3 months indicated 40% of the applications took more than 2 days for processing. It was found that each application was travelling in batches and required more than 100 meters for completion of its process.

The level of WIP discovered due to duplication of work at each stage was high. This resulted in a financial loss to the company as well as potential threat of losing the business to competitors. Also, the number of complaints received for incorrect card details was significant which added in rework and customer dissatisfaction. The process cycle efficiency was measured as 1.45%.

Relevant process KPI:

TAT for processing application – Goal was 1.5 day

How was it solved?

Batch processing was eliminated by the introduction of single-piece flow. Identification of locations receiving a significant number of applications was done which were upgraded with the technology to introduce single-piece flow.

Value analysis was conducted to eradicate non-value adding activities and duplication of work

The cell was re-designed to create a proper cell layout, allow a continuous flow of all the applications and reduce

Standard operating procedures were laid out to eliminate errors and reduce the variation in the process

What are the benefits?

The average time for the process has been reduced to 1.5 days. Process cycle efficiency has been increased to 99.9997%. Removal of non-value adding activities has reduced the total number of activities to 29 as on previous 67. Also re-designing the cell has truncated the distance travelled by the documents to 20 meters. Dening standard work has doubled the productivity per person reducing the percentage of rework to 0.2%.

Case Study – 2

Project Title: Improving TAT and accuracy of the payment process

Scenario

LB Inc is a multi-National company. It purchases products and services from its different vendors. The payment process involving the calculation of service tax, TDS, Internal order are being outsourced to R. K. Group. It does all the calculations pertaining to purchased product or service and prepares cheque or ECS and is sent back to LB's Accounts Manager and Finance Director. Payment to R. K. Group happens on the number of transactions processed accurately and loses business opportunity for every defective transaction passed on to LB's Vendor. The lost business opportunity costs to the tune of Rs 100 for every defective transaction.

What was the problem?

The monthly report for defects reported that only 30% of the payments were timely and accurate. The majority of the defects were found in name of the vendor, TDS calculation and amount entered on the cheque. The process cycle efficiency calculated for the quarter was around 65%. Approval at several stages of payment implied the lead time for the process which also influenced the service levels.

The average turnaround time for each payment was calculated as 5 days against the service levels of 2 days. The target was to reduce inaccuracy level below 0.1% in a period of 3 months and an average cycle time of 1.5 days.

Relevant process KPI:

TAT for processing payment – Goal was 1.5 day

How was it solved

Process re-engineering has eliminated multiple approvals and reduced work in progress which increased the cycle time. Once layout was restructured to ensure that all payments are process as a single piece and batching was restricted. Appropriate resource distribution was done to contribute resources at required process steps. Defects in names and TDS calculation have been eliminated by automation. Automation has cut-down many non-value adding activities contributing to pace up the processing time.

What are the benefits

The number of payments processed has increased from 100 to 175 per day in a period of 3 months. Automation of the process has eliminated many nonvalue adding activities reducing the number of process steps from 63 to 15 and distance travelled by the documents to 25 meters. The goal of reducing the cycle time to 1.5 days has been achieved. A rolled throughput yield of 99.97% has been achieved within a quarter.

The intangible benefits include customer goodwill and loyalty which has improved the reliability.

Case Study – 3

Project Title: Improve Productivity and reduce Inventory.

Scenario:

MNC Ltd is a Small-Scale Industry engaged in the manufacturing of printed circuit boards for various applications. It has been facing heavy competition although having market demand twice as much as it can produce. Like any other typical manufacturing company, they had space constraints due to which all manufacturing processes were arranged in three adjacent plots.

What was the problem?

MNC Ltd was having a process layout like any other manufacturing company, arranging the machines based on the manufacturing steps such as cutting, drilling, screen printing, etching, etc. It was carrying high inventory to the tune of 10-15 days of production. Due to poor housekeeping & jumbled up layout, there was no traceability of the material and with the fragmented layout there was no accountability of people and material, leading to profit leakages, resulting from scrap, re-work & excessive inventories.

As the material was not flowing smoothly the MNC Ltd management has to grant over time during the last 10 days of every month in order to clear back lock of sales order resulting in erosion of profits. Since the manufacturing operations are fragmented and due to lack of accountability for the output, the senior management of MNC Ltd has to co-ordinate between the various processes.

Relevant Process KPI:

WIP Inventory was 10-15 days and the goal was to reduce it to 2 days.

How was it solved?

1. Analysis of their current work ow from the raw material to finished goods and data of the cycle time of every process, inventory as WIP, machine down time, change over time from one model to another & rejection, rework level and focus areas were identified for improvement.

2. Re-engineering the process flow from '2. Push System' to 'Pull System' in which the raw material will flow into small batches from one manufacturing process to another without waiting as WIP.

3. Establish visual controls such as quantity planned, quantity 3. produced, Kanban system to communicate between one stage of manufacturing to another to ensure that the raw material converted into finished goods sold on the same day

Using the above approach, the Lean system was implemented within 60 days of the commencement of the project.

What are the benefits?

1. Productivity Improvement

MNC Ltd.'s productivity has gone up from 2 lac PCB/month to 6 lac PCB/ month without any capital investment. This is a result of the smooth & continuous flow of material due to the 'Pull System' introduced.

2. Inventory Reduction

The Lean manufacturing system introduced at Skylark has brought down the WIP inventory from 15 days to 2 days dramatically reducing the working capital for running the business

3. Reduction in Floor Space

The cell manufacturing layout introduced at Skylark to facilitate continuous & smooth flow of material & reduction of inventory has relieved 20% of the floor space which can be utilized for better purpose.

4. Improved Profitability

The profitability has gone up by 5 times due to increase sales, reduced inventory, reduction in overtime charges & reduction in rejection & rework.

Index

The following flowchart summarizes the entire RAMOR for easy reference:

Enigma of Lean

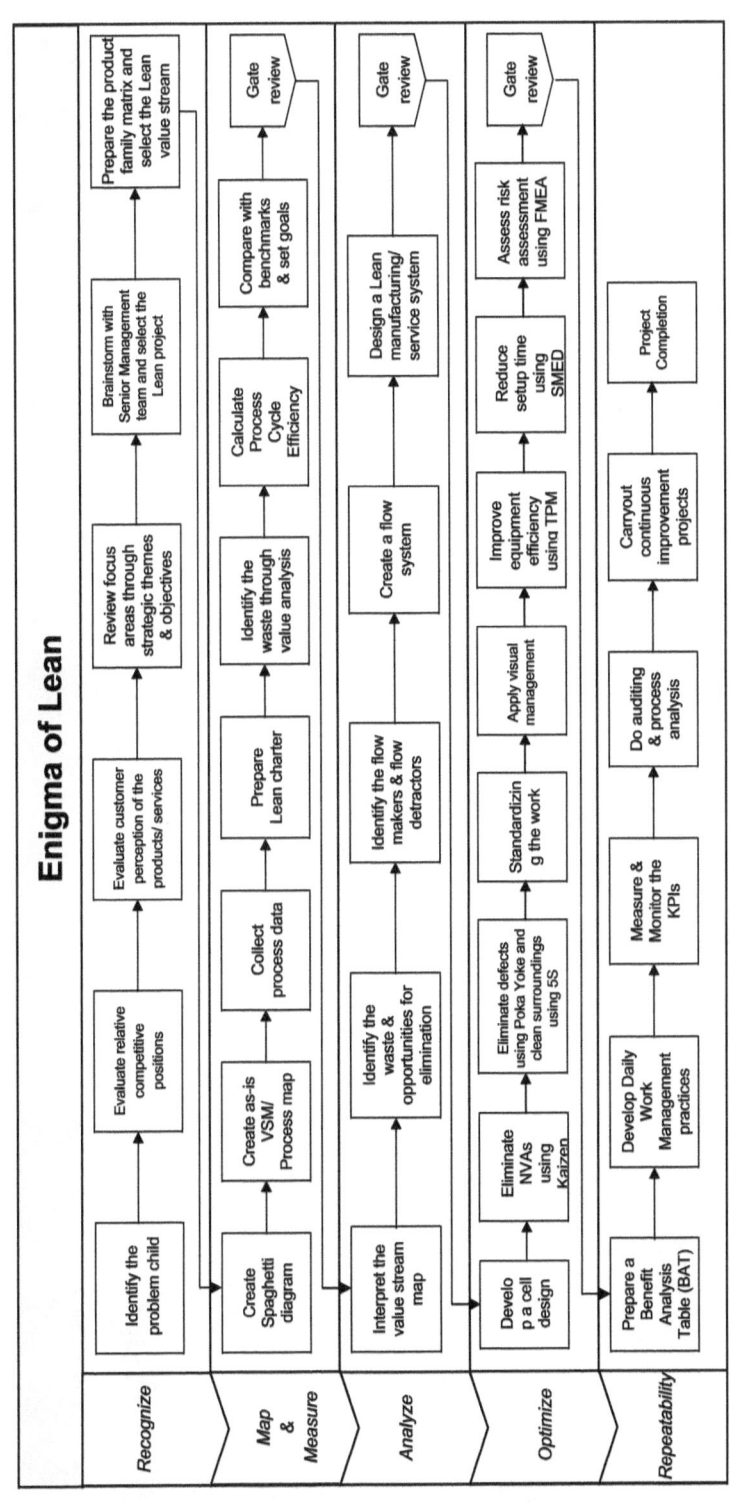

END OF THE BOOK